Suffering Well

How to Steward God's Most Feared Blessing

Rick Thomas

The Counseling Solutions Group, Inc.

Copyright

Suffering Well – How to Steward God's Most Feared Blessing

ISBN: 978-1-7323854-1-2

LCCN: 2018907454

Cover Artwork by: Elieser Loewenthal

Edited by: Sarah Hayhurst

Edited by: Rachel Huerta

© 2018 by Rick Thomas

Published by The Counseling Solutions Group, Inc.

120 Goodridge Court

Greer, SC 29651

RickThomas.Net

Printed in the United States of America.

Dedication

To Job

"For the thing that I fear comes upon me,

and what I dread befalls me" (Job 3:25).

Endorsements

"Rick Thomas invites his readers to enter into a place for "mature audiences" only, to listen as he recounts the darkest time in his life and how, through his journey of intense suffering, he was led to spend four years in the Book of Job.

What he discovered was that the book wasn't really about Job (the most famous sufferer of all time) – but about God, and in particular – about learning to trust God in all our circumstances. This book is especially rich with biblical references to support his conclusions on why we are "called" to suffer.

Consistent with his biblical counseling background, Rick gives the reader specific calls to action at the end of each chapter, making it not only an engaging read but practical as well. The book can be used for personal devotions, used in a small group setting or given away as a gift – it will bless the giver and the receiver!"

Nancy Hohmann, Enid, Oklahoma

"For the thing that I fear comes upon me, and what I dread befalls me (Job 3:25). What then? There is generally a lot of talk regarding the benefits of salvation through Christ, but very little regarding the benefits of suffering.

This book takes you from the beginning of Job's and the author's stories (terrible loss), through God's purpose (making us more like Christ), to the end (forgiveness on our part, followed by restoration). I used the questions and calls to action and was able to apply what I was reading to my own life.

I learned that suffering is not meaningless. There is a powerful beauty in working with God through times of suffering, for our good and His glory. The blessing of suffering will help me die to myself and get closer to God. I'm grateful to have my eyes opened to this facet of the faith in such a practical way.

I can approach suffering differently in the future by keeping my eyes on God and what He's trying to accomplish. Read this book. There are lessons there for anyone earnestly seeking God."

Pat Wolff, Greenville, South Carolina

One thing is for certain, I have often identified with suffering. Disturbingly, I would even go as far as claiming to be a professional pain and sorrow image bearer. Yet, I was quickly reminded through reading this book that as much as I suffered in my lifetime, I was not "suffering well."

"Suffering Well" was more than just a great read; this was personal. By page 10, God had gently navigated me back to Job's stoop without me knowing it. As I reluctantly knocked on his door, he lovingly invited me in for tea and shared his journey of sanctification with me once again.

At times I cringed, laughed, wanted to turn away, and even flee at the parts in his story that seemed to parallel mine. Nonetheless, as painful as it was to sip my tea and see my reflection in my cup now full of humble tears, I could not resist turning the pages as God was showing me it was now time to "suffer well." Thank you for the tea.

Alana Altitude, San Francisco, California

Human nature despises suffering, and yet, as Rick Thomas emphasizes in his book, Suffering Well, suffering is a gift from God intended for our good and God's glory.

In truth, to follow Christ and to enjoy His presence is to join with Him in His suffering. This book is not simply a theology of suffering—though Rick covers this important starting point well; it is also a practical work that will greatly benefit the believer. More specifically, the book presents biblical truths that will enable readers to know God's goodness and sovereignty more clearly and to grow in their faith more intimately when they encounter various trials and tribulations.

Moreover, the counsel Rick gives is not theory or man's wisdom apart from the gospel. Instead, Rick offers a unique perspective: God's wisdom which personally enabled his growth during one of the greatest times of suffering in his own life. I highly recommend that you purchase a copy, read and reread this relevant book, and then share it with other believers who are suffering.

Dr. Daniel Berger, Taylors, South Carolina

Table of Contents

The Worst Day

On April 8, 1988, it all went wrong. I would soon call that day the "beginning of woes." I walked into my home shortly past 5 o'clock, after a full day at work, and noticed the missing piano in our living room. I immediately knew what had happened. My wife of nine years decided she had enough: it was time to leave. A simple note left on the kitchen table. It read,

"You're right; we can't go on like this. I'll call you later."

I had shared that sentiment earlier, not knowing how it would haunt me for years to come. We had been having on again, off again arguments for over three years. I don't have any valid answer for why we were arguing except to say we both were selfish, young, and ignorant. Somehow, in some way, we went off the tracks, and for reasons that I don't fully understand, we could never make it right.

We had moved to Greenville, South Carolina, two years earlier so I could attend a small Bible college. My thought was that God wanted me to go into full-time Christian ministry. My wife was happy about this decision and had helped me to make it. Our church was supportive and encouraged us to go. They graciously paid for my tuition.

It seemed to be the right thing to do, and looking back on it, I believe this was God's pleasure and direction for our lives. It made sense then and now. But from 1988 to 1997 it made little sense as I lived in a continual state of confusion.

In the Beginning

Before marriage, we were not Christians. In 1979 we eloped. We bought a small mobile home and placed it on 3.42 acres that we had paid for before marriage. Five years later, the Father mercifully came into my life and saved me. Though we were not "bad" people, salvation was a new beginning for us.

We were your typical, countrified Southern family. We went to the local fish camp on Friday night, worked in the yard all day on Saturday, and would go to our local church two times on Sunday and, of course, Wednesday night, too. We had two children: a girl born in 1981 and a boy born in 1983. We were living the all-American dream.

After arriving in Greenville in 1986, we set up camp and began our brand-new college experience. We were both twenty-six years old. I was working full-time during the day at a local recycling factory while going to school full-time, Monday through Friday, during the evenings. Sadly, I did not see a problem with our marriage. Our pastor in Greenville taught us, "You take care of God's business, and He will take care of yours." I believed him, so I poured everything I had into taking care of the Lord's business.

I learned two years later that God did not take care of my business as I sat in an empty house wondering where it all went wrong. One of the things the Father taught me in the years to come was that "taking care of His business" also meant my family. I had bought into a one-sided notion that ministry was exclusively outside of the family.

Mounting Trouble

Things seemed to be going well for the most part except for the on-going, low-grade arguing that came in and out of our lives. It was rarely anything major, but it never corrected either.

One of the contributing factors was in June of 1987, a year after our arrival in Greenville, I received one of those dreadful phone calls that no one wants to accept. My mother called to tell me that my oldest brother had been murdered in an argument. He went to prison when he was about seventeen years old and had been in and out of jail from that time until he was murdered fifteen years later.

He had gotten into an argument and was shot twice in the head with a double-barrel shotgun. The assailant took the barrel of the gun and used it as a sledgehammer to crush my brother's skull.

My brother had just gotten out of prison in January for the third time, but per his usual, he would not avoid trouble. He was what you would call an "institutionalized convict." He had been in so long that he had a hard time living on the outside. He would do things that would get him locked up.

The last time I saw him alive was on Easter Sunday in April 1987. He came to our local church meeting. I noticed toward the end of the meeting that he was noticeably shaken as he was processing the message. It was one of those rare moments for a convict who had learned how to "be all things to all people." This time he could not hide his fears.

I went to him and asked if he wanted to become a Christian. I told him that it seemed apparent that God was working in his life and he needed to trust Him. I asked him if he understood what the preacher was saying. He said that he did, but he could not be saved today because there were "some things he needed to do." That was that, and the last time I saw him alive.

We came back to Greenville, and I did not return home until my mother's phone call in June. It took a while to process those events. My wife said they changed me. She was probably right. It was a hard summer, our second year in Greenville.

It was also during the summer of 1987 when she began seeing another man. I did not know this until a year later. She told me the following summer, a few months after she left. They worked together. He was married. I'm not sure how long that relationship lasted. By the time April 1988 had rolled around, she had made her decision to move out and take our children with her.

"But he is unchangeable, and who can turn him back? What he desires, that he does. For he will complete what he appoints for me, and many such things are in his mind" (Job 23:13–14).

Believing that God would never allow a divorce because He hates it, I did not press the issue of who should keep the children until our problems were solved. Regrettably, I wish I had gotten the kids and filed for legal custody, but thinking we would never be divorced, I let her keep them during the separation period. When we finally went to court two years later, the judge awarded the kids to their mother for two reasons. The children had been with their mother the past two years, and he did not want to uproot them again.

He said that their lives were complicated enough, and since they had been with her, he did not want to disrupt their situation again. Though it sounded like sound wisdom, I disagreed. As the years have shown, it was an unwise decision.

The judge also said that he did not see a Christian upbringing as anything special. A significant point of my argument in the child custody battle was the merits of a Christian family versus a non-Christian one. He was not convinced, as he determined to award our children to my newly legalized ex-wife.

It was a sunny day.

I remember stepping out on the courthouse steps in Greenville, South Carolina, looking up into the bright, beautiful, blue sky and weeping. It was final. I lost my wife and two children on that lovely fall day.

God hates divorce, and my hatred for it was growing by the minute. I was stunned. I could not believe what just happened. Why would God permit this to happen? The judge silenced two years of praying, asking, working, begging, and pleading when he slammed his gavel on the bench. I learned on that day how truth and a court of law do not necessarily coexist.

For the record, he asked me what I wanted to do. I told him that I wanted to reconcile with my wife. He then asked if I was aware of her position, that she wanted a divorce. I said to him that I was aware of her perspective, but I wanted it as a matter of court record: I disagreed that our marriage could not change, and regardless of the opinion of the court, I was against the divorce. He made it a matter of court record.

I was divorced.

Back to the Beginning

When I walked into the living room of my home on April 8, I immediately went running through the house looking for my family. Though there was no warning, I knew what had happened: my family was gone! I cannot explain to you what exactly happened in my mind on that day other than to say that I lost it. The few things I remember about my evening are imprinted on my memory. As for the forgotten things, they are only in the mind of God.

Upon seeing the piano missing, I sprinted toward the bedrooms, looking in the corners and closets for my wife and kids. She did not take everything—only personal belongings, beds, some furniture, and a few other things. The kid's bedrooms were empty. I went on a frantic search for my family. I began looking in the closets and under my bed. Yes, in the drawers, too. I remember going into the kitchen, looking through the cupboards and drawers, but to no avail. My family was not in the house. They were gone, and I knew they were not coming back anytime soon.

From the kitchen, I ran into the hallway and fell prostrate on the floor. I could hardly breathe. I was trying to catch my breath, huffing from the depths of my soul. It was more like a gasp or bellow or some sad, hollow sound. I could not cry. I later called it "beyond tears." The agony and terror transcended my impotent tears.

Oddly enough, I was a stoic person before my wife left, rarely showing emotion. I had learned a long time ago not to let my feelings known to others because weakness was unacceptable. On April 8, 1988, God broke my heart. I have not stopped crying since that dreadful day.

The last thing I remember from my first Friday alone was sitting on the floor of my living room around 10 p.m. I opened my Bible to Psalm 51, not because of the point of the Psalm, David's adultery with Bathsheba, but because I knew the first two words. I wanted to read them. I wanted to look at them. I wanted those first two words to soak deeply into my soul. I needed healing and those words were perfect for me, so I opened my Bible to that blessed Psalm and uttered those first two words.

"Have mercy."

I fell over on the floor, and that was the last thing I remember from that night. When I awoke the next morning, I was in my bed. I have no idea how that happened. I went to work that Saturday morning. My routine was to weigh myself on the floor scales in our plant. When I left the plant at 5 p.m. on Friday, I weighed 168 pounds. Fifteen hours later, just before 8 a.m. on Saturday, I weighed 158 pounds. This was the beginning of woes.

The separation and the divorce started the Lord's merciful "divine deconstruction." There was more. The company that I was working for started phasing out their plants around the country. Ours was on the list. They shut down our office, and I was on the street. There was no notice. The District Manager came, and we were out of the plant in less than two hours. I was the plant manager.

Within two years I lost my wife, children, and job. We also had to liquidate the property that we had held in North Carolina after we moved to Greenville. I was broke and no longer able to afford our rental in Greenville.

The possibility of being a pastor was out the window too. I belonged to a slice of Christianity called "Fundamentalism." This legalistic demographic has a "one strike, you're out policy" as it pertains to a divorced person being in ministry. They told me that I could tell people about Jesus, but I could not preach to anyone about Jesus. They disqualified me from Christian ministry. The life I expected when I moved to Greenville vaporized on April 8.

A college friend told me about a lady who owned a dilapidated mobile home along a tree line in a pasture that I could rent for $125 per month. He had just moved back home to Hattiesburg, Mississippi. Without a place to stay and no job or income, I took it and spent the next four years in that trailer. I began picking up aluminum cans to sell. It was in this context that I embarked on a four-year experiential study in the Book of Job.

"The Spirit immediately drove him out into the wilderness. And he was in the wilderness forty days, being tempted by Satan. And he was with the wild animals, and the angels were ministering to him" (Mark 1:11–12).

After meeting God in "my wilderness," I began to see His purposes with a new set of eyes. He was creatively working in me to bring shape to my "theology of suffering worldview" (Philippians 2:12–13). Before He could use me, He had to change me. How could I

14

serve Him well in His world without walking in the steps of Jesus? I did not understand these things then, but I see them clearly now.

"I had heard of you by the hearing of the ear, but now my eye sees you; therefore I despise myself, and repent in dust and ashes" (Job 42:5–6).

The Lord took away everything that was dear to me. I was single, fatherless, and penniless, with no future hope of restoration on any front or even a future that would be any different from my present darkness. The pain was so profound that I could feel it.

There is a "normal" darkness that can come over the soul, and there is a darkness of the soul that can be felt deeply (Exodus 10:21). This latter darkness transcends words. Sublunary language never reaches the height or the depth of that darkness. You feel it though you can't articulate it. It's deeper than deep (Psalm 42:7), of which there is only one cure. You must die (Matthew 16:24).

"Truly, truly, I say to you, unless a grain of wheat falls into the earth and dies, it remains alone; but if it dies, it bears much fruit" (John 12:24).

But If It Dies

What I could not see, what I was afraid to see, and what I refused to see was how the Lord was in my suffering. I did not want to perceive Him. To look at God in the crucible of suffering was to stare into my death (Luke 22:42). That is when it first dawned on me what He was up to. Here is my epiphany: He had a Son, and it was His pleasure to crush Him. "Yet it was the will of the Lord to crush him; he has put him to grief" (Isaiah 53:10). Now I'm one of His sons.

"See what kind of love the Father has given to us, that we should be called children of God; and so we are" (1 John 3:1).

Why should I consider it a strange thing (1 Peter 4:12) for my Father to make me walk in the steps of His beloved Son (1 Peter 2:21). I asked Him to forgive me for my stubborn, self-righteous anger that was demanding He see and do things my way. He forgave me.

But nothing changed, except I seemed to perceive a sprinkle of hope coming like a small cloud forming in the sky about the size of a man's hand (1 Kings 18:43–44). Eventually, the rain came. And when it did, the Lord reaffirmed that what He started at salvation, He was going to complete (Philippians 1:6).

In His mysterious timing, He equipped and released me to serve others. This book is the fruit of what He taught me during those dark days. Thank you for reading it. You are one of the persons the Lord had in mind when He called me on April 8, 1988, to walk in the suffering steps of Jesus.

"For to this you have been called, because Christ also suffered for you, leaving you an example, so that you might follow in his steps" (1 Peter 2:21).

Debtor to mercy,
Rick
Greenville, South Carolina
April 8, 2018

A Short Primer on Suffering

We can agree on this: personal suffering is the one thing we fear the most. Think about it for a minute. Certain things come to mind that tempt you to fear. Maybe you don't spend a lot of time thinking about it, and that is probably good. If you do think about your fear, if only for a moment, you know that you fear something.

- What if the thing you feared came true?
- What if personal suffering did come to your life?
- How would you respond?

Job put it this way:

"For the thing that I fear comes upon me, and what I dread befalls me" (Job 3:25).

Prayers Answered through Suffering

Mable prayed for thirteen years that her marriage would change. She prayed more specifically that her husband would transform. Biff was a half-hearted husband as well as a half-hearted Christian. The primary emphasis in his life had been to work hard and long hours. If you asked him, he would say that he was a good husband because he provided for his family.

The "providing for the family" card is one of the most over-used, sinful justifications for the man who chooses to be a lousy husband. He decides to get his love cup filled by finding his identity in his work.

As the years rolled on, the work hours became longer, and their marital distance grew wider. Mable knew there was more to the story, but she could not put two and two together. Then her suspicions were validated when a text from Biff inadvertently went to Mable's phone. He meant it for a female colleague three states away.

Mable's initial confrontation with her husband was fruitless as he denied her accusations. Biff was feeling her out. He was trying to discern how much she knew and how much he should tell. Once he knew the evidence was irrefutable, he came clean about his nineteen-month affair.

Though the counseling took several months and there were many ups and downs along the way, Biff repented authentically, and Mable came to a gospel-centered, sovereign view of suffering that released her to forgive her husband freely and to pursue genuine reconciliation.

Mable's prayers for a good marriage were answered but only through the crucible of extreme suffering.

For Mature Audiences Only

The remainder of this chapter will be speaking to this kind of high-level, mature Christian response to personal suffering; the type Mable was called to endure. It could be that you have not come to this place in your "theology of suffering." Do not be discouraged. Be prayerful and ask God to give you the grace to understand what is written here so that you can adequately steward this "most-feared gift."

Your suffering, no matter what it is, did not come to you without God's allowance as well as His mysterious concern for you. The primary aspect you must work through is between you, the sufferer, and God.

If you don't do this, you'll not be able to come to a right perspective on your suffering. Suffering is inevitable for every human. It is unavoidable. Suffering is an imminent and painful reality, which is why it is all the more important that you see suffering through the lens of God's sovereign plan for your life.

"When pain is to be borne, a little courage helps more than much knowledge, a little human sympathy more than much courage, and the least tincture of the love of God more than all." —C.S. Lewis

Before Mable could adequately work through what was going on in her marriage, she had to have her heart adjusted by her kind and loving heavenly Father. There is a progression through pain, and Mable needed to understand these concepts. This short primer presents eight aspects that set the stage to follow in the steps of the Savior.

The Progression of Pain

It's Time to Die

"Truly, truly, I say to you, unless a grain of wheat falls into the earth and dies, it remains alone; but if it dies, it bears much fruit" (John 12:24).

The Savior is teaching us that the only way we can live is by dying. Fruit bearing comes through the door of death. There is no other way if your hope and desire are to be fruitful. I am not trying to be mean or unsympathetic toward what is happening to you. Truths about suffering are hard.

Part of the maturing process has to include a purifying process because the truth is that we have many ways, attitudes, and patterns in our lives that need changing. A picture of mercy from the Lord is Him loving us enough to purify us by removing things from our lives that hinder us from knowing Him more profoundly.

It's Time to Participate

"That I may know him and the power of his resurrection and may share his sufferings, becoming like him in his death" (Philippians 3:10).

Knowing Christ is an expensive, challenging, and painful process, and it will cost you your life—do not be deceived about this. Do you want to know Christ? If so, you must understand Him. He was a man of sorrows and acquainted with grief. He was despised and rejected of men (Isaiah 53). Do you think you can "know" Him in a detached and unaffected way? No. Never. Not in this life.

If you are a person who loves the Savior and you desire to know Him genuinely, there is no other choice for you but to share in the fellowship of His sufferings. You cannot participate in the power of His resurrection until you engage in His sufferings.

"For it has been granted to you that for the sake of Christ you should not only believe in him but also suffer for his sake" (Philippians 1:29).

There are two gifts that you receive as a Christian. The first is the gift of salvation. When you first encounter God in a salvific way, He grants you the gift of salvation. To be born again is a beautiful thing.

But salvation is not the only gift under the "Christmas tree." Imagine gathering around the tree this Christmas, and, to your delight, you discover there are two gifts for you. You open the first and find out you have been born from above. Joy! Then you ask,

"What is that second gift under the tree?"

That gift, my friend, is the gift of suffering. This truth is the point of Philippians 1:29. God gives all Christians at least two gifts: (1) salvation and (2) suffering. I'm well aware this is not a good "Evangelism 101" approach:

"Hey, you wanna suffer? Become a Christian."

We typically leave out the suffering part, though we should not. We should be more forthright with what it means to become a Christian: the more serious you take your faith, the more you will suffer. The Bible could not be more explicit.

It's Time to Follow

"For to this, you have been called, because Christ also suffered for you, leaving you an example, so that you might follow in his steps" (Peter 2:21).

To suffer is part of the calling of every Christian. Have you ever wondered what your calling is in life? I'm not sure of all God has called you to, but I do know this much: He has called you and me as believers to suffer. The word Christian means Christ follower. Part of the life of a Christ follower is suffering.

It's Time to See

"See what kind of love the Father has given to us, that we should be called children of God; and so we are" (1 John 3:1).

In 2015, my doctor put stitches on the top of my head. Why did he do this? In part, because he loves me. He cares about my health, so he asked if he could cut a small growth from my head so that he could have it checked. The process was somewhat painful, though not nearly as painful as many other procedures that happen to people. Sometimes love means I must be hurt to find help. You need to know this about our loving heavenly Father.

Sometimes the "manner of love" He bestows upon us is in a package we might not initially understand as "love" and most probably not embrace as love. What did John tell us in another place? God so loved us that He (executed) His one and only Son (John 3:16). Our Father is a radical lover.

It's Time to Experience

"Yet it was the will of the LORD to crush him; he has put him to grief" (Isaiah 53:10).

If the Father believed it necessary to crush His one and only Son to save you and me, do you think His love for us will always be soft carpet, stocked pantries, and clean beds?

"You will not get leave to steal quietly to heaven, in Christ's company, without a conflict and a cross." —Samuel Rutherford

Sometimes the love of God will crush us. The billows will come over us, and we'll be so disoriented that the love of God will be the furthest thing from our minds.

It's Time to Realize

"Where were you when I laid the foundation of the earth? Tell me, if you have understanding" (Job 38:42).

Though Job understood, to a degree, what was happening to him, he did not entirely get it until the very end of the book that carries his name. Before the turning (or restoring) of his captivity, God stepped in and gave Job some counsel. God was lovingly hard on Job as he put him in his place. Job had become way too whiny, entitled, and disgruntled about what was happening to him. This response to God is also my danger. At times I forget my place. I think I deserve better than what I have, regardless of what I have. I forget that I was a rebel before

God, bound for hell. Sometimes I think that I am somebody when I unleash my arrogance and begin to prance around like I deserve better.

As painful as it is, it is a mercy of the Lord to put me in my place. Biblically, I cannot say the unpleasant things that have happened to me were not a mercy of the Lord. Though there have been many harsh, hard, and unkind things done to me, I do understand the helping and loving hand of God in all of it.

Will You Die?

"I had heard of you by the hearing of the ear, but now my eye sees you; therefore I despise myself and repent in dust and ashes" (Job 42:5–6).

Job got it. He finally understood. God stood on Job's neck for four chapters (38–41), hardly letting up at all, and the scales eventually fell from Job's eyes. Formerly, he had heard of God, but now, in the context of personal suffering and stern counsel from the Lord, he found his place with God. He was rightly and wholly affected by his loving Father.

Honestly, what God did appears to be a divine beat down. The force of God's words put Job in his place, and Job was "dead." The grain of wheat had entirely fallen into the ground (John 12:24), and Job died to himself. Though he did not know it, he was only a few moments away from an incredible blessing. God was about to turn things around for His friend.

"And the LORD restored the fortunes of Job when he had prayed for his friends. And the LORD gave Job twice as much as he had before" (Job 42:10).

The big word in this text is "when." God turned Job's captivity "when" he prayed for his friends. The word "when" means an element of time. God turned Job's captivity "when" Job came to that time in his heart where he could freely intercede for those who had hurt him. Can you do this? This kind of praying is not intellectual assent. It is purified praying from a broken and contrite heart (Psalm 51:17).

Maybe you need to ask God to do more work in your heart. Ask God to give you the grace that will enable you to pray and serve those who have hurt you. "When" you can do this, you can expect God's inestimable favor to flood your life and soul.

Proceed with Caution

Initially, Mable was not able to process, understand, and most definitely apply what I am saying here. She was too hurt, too angry, and too unforgiving. I also knew she would be too offended if I brought these more profound truths to her attention. This view of suffering is only for mature audiences. I had to be very patient with Mable. Sometimes the best words are not said at the best times.

She was not able to see that what was happening to her was a carefully prepared blessing from her loving heavenly Father. In time, she understood. In time, she experienced a more profound grace from God than what most of us know. Think about how difficult it was for the Savior to fully embrace the crushing from His Father, the crushing that God planned in eternity past. We sing about it and call it "amazing love," but it was amazingly hard for Him to die.

"My soul is very sorrowful, even to death; remain here, and watch with me." And going a little farther he fell on his face and prayed, saying, "My Father, if it be possible, let this cup pass from me; nevertheless, not as I will, but as you will" (Matthew 26:38–39).

Mable was not initially able to steward God's most-feared blessing. Mable had been praying for a biblical marriage for thirteen years, but she could never have a biblical marriage because her husband did not have a heart for God—he had a heart for himself.

Though Mable would have been happier if Biff would have repented without an affair, she began to understand that God's method to bring Biff back to her was needful on many different levels.

Biff was not only dissing Mable, but he was trashing God's name. God is a jealous God, and Biff professed to be His son. God would not allow Biff to continue on the path that he was going. Not only did God answer Mable's prayer by giving her the biblical marriage that she longed for, but He made a significant correction in Biff's heart. He repented of his sin and began the long process of restoring his relationship with God and with his wife.

My hope and prayer for the Mable's of this world are that they will be able to embrace and appropriate God's grace in their lives, especially when their time of suffering comes. To do this, they must come to the place of understanding what is happening to them in their horizontal world is not the main issue.

It is what God is doing in their vertical worlds that needs addressing first. The pain from others is profound. The physical suffering we endure due to our weaknesses is mysterious. No matter how hurt and suffering come our way, it is essential that we see and understand how God's love is working through that pain is the victory.

"And whoever does not take his cross and follow me is not worthy of me. Whoever finds his life will lose it, and whoever loses his life for my sake will find it" (Matthew 10:39–40).

Without a doubt, suffering is God's most-feared blessing. And as odd as it may sound, it is a gift—a gift to be stewarded. How are you stewarding the gift? The remainder of this book will delve into the mystery of Job's suffering and how God used this gift to bring our old friend into a more in-depth and satisfying relationship with his Maker.

Chapter 1

Four Things to Know

Religion could be an enjoyable experience if suffering were not part of our lives. The pain was my biggest disappointment and greatest frustration after becoming a Christian. Though living a traumatic childhood was unbearable at times, it did not seem odd to me because I lived in a family that did not love God. Bad things happen to bad people, right? It was the disappointment of suffering after being regenerated that was hard to swallow.

"We were promised sufferings. They were part of the program. We were even told, 'Blessed are they that mourn,' and I accept it. I've got nothing that I hadn't bargained for. Of course, it is different when the thing happens to oneself, not to others, and in reality, not imagination." —C. S. Lewis

Bad things happen to bad people, but bad things should not happen to people who are trying to do good. Depending on how thick that theological misthinking weaves itself into the fabric of your view of God will determine the amount of disappointment you experience when hard things come your way. The patriarch of suffering in the Bible is Job. He did nothing to deserve what happened to him. Though he knew that he was not sinless, Job did not believe he deserved his devastation. And to make matters worse was the deafening silence of God.

"Behold, I go forward, but he is not there, and backward, but I do not perceive him; on the left hand when he is working, I do not behold him; he turns to the right hand, but I do not see him" (Job 23:8–9).

Have you been to that spot in your life where the trouble came and God was silent? Strapped in a straitjacket and dropped into an ocean of suffering is one of the most hopeless experiences in life. Our brother Job was in that place.

He lived his life according to the rules, not because he was a legalist but because he loved God. If Job had died in the first chapter of his book, we would testify that he was a good man who loved the Lord. He was a man of integrity (Job 1:1). The first part of his experience could be summed up in six descending steps.

1. I was trying to do good.
2. Trouble came into my life.
3. I did not deserve the trouble.
4. I began to fall apart.
5. None of it made sense.
6. And there was no one there to comfort me—not even the Lord.

Have you ever been in a similar place where your suffering did not make sense, and the Lord was not forthcoming with a reason or a solution? If you have, you more than likely have had similar questions running through your head:

- What kind of God runs the world this way?
- What kind of God governs our lives in a seemingly uncaring way?
- How are we supposed to think about God when a person experiences undeserved suffering?

One of the most critical aspects of our suffering is how we think about God when the pain comes. To miss this point of suffering is to mishandle and misunderstand what is happening to you. Suffering can be a means of grace to help us rethink about how we think about God. If our focus is more on our pain than the God who is allowing the suffering, we do not understand God or suffering correctly.

Just in Case

"And when the days of the feast had run their course, Job would send and consecrate them, and he would rise early in the morning and offer burnt offerings according to the number of them all. For Job said, 'It may be that my children have sinned, and cursed God in their hearts.' Thus Job did continually" (Job 1:5).

Verse five is an insightful verse that could be a linchpin that holds one of the central mysteries of the book. When Job considered the possibility of his children sinning against God, he decided to offer sacrifices on their behalf. He did this continually.

This act from Job was more of a reflection on how he thought about God than how he felt about his children. And that "legalistic perspective" was most definitely the accusation of Satan.

"Does Job fear God for no reason? Have you not put a hedge around him and his house and all that he has, on every side? You have blessed the work of his hands, and his possessions have increased in the land" (Job 1:9–10).

I think if I observed Job's life, I would conclude two big things from the first five verses: (1) Job loves God, but (2) I wonder if he fully trusts God the right way. Nobody questions Job's love for the Lord or his desire to serve him. Brother Job was a man of spotless character and deep affection for his Lord.

The real question is whether or not Job was perfect. We already know the answer to that question. Job was like us in that way. He was a flawed man—he was an Adamic man, which we see in verse five.

With all our faith and with all His grace, we still want to maintain some feeling of control over our lives. Maybe Job's theology was colored by his culture. I do not know. The land of Uz was not in Israel. He lived in a predominantly pagan land. Every other deity in his culture believed they had to appease a god. Most certainly our Adamic tendencies are to please God by our works. We are all legalists to a degree.

Part of the mentality of the legalist is an "other shoe is going to drop" worldview. They strive to be holy because they have an awkward understanding of obedience. Conversely, we know the prosperity gospel folks have a terrible theological formula, too: if I do well, the Lord will bless me.

What about you? You are not a legalist, and you are not a prosperity person, but wouldn't you agree that there are traces in your theology that has an "I must work to please God" mentality? If you do well, the Lord will bless, and if you do not well, the Lord will not bless. I counsel people like this all the time. Here are a few manifestations:

- I missed my daily Bible study, and something terrible happened to me. I see a direct correlation between my lack of devotions and the trouble in my life.
- My child is not walking with the Lord, and I was not a good parent. If I had been a better parent, the Lord would have motivated my child to love and follow Him.
- I am stuck in habitual sin. I know the Lord is going to get me for this. I live under the unrelenting cloud that expects God to do something terrible to my family or me.
- We fornicated while we were dating, and now we have a miserable marriage. The Lord is punishing us. You reap what you sow, you know? We are receiving the fruit of our actions.
- If I "go to church," my children will be okay. I connect the chances of the Lord blessing us with good kids to our church attendance.

I doubt there is a person who is reading this that has not thought like this to some degree. You may not be as righteous as Job, but there is a part of you that does question God's love and good intentions for you. I know I am this way. We all have a little bit of legalism in us. It is part of our fallenness.

Serving a Formulaic Lord

Some will argue that you do reap what you sow (Galatians 6:7), which is correct. It is also common sense. If you plant to the flesh, the chances of you reaping corruption are high. But may I caution you to put guardrails on that kind of thinking?

All of us sow to the flesh in some way. Which one of us does not struggle with a lifelong, habitual sin pattern like anger or worry or fear or lust? God is a merciful God, who does not deal with us according to His law. You do not reap all that you sow.

The "if I do this and God will do that" theology is reducing the Lord to a formula. This formulaic view of God will run you into a deep hole of works and fear. One of the most important things you can do when personal suffering comes into your life is to reexamine how you think about God.

"What comes into our minds when we think about God is the most important thing about us." —A. W. Tozer

How can we ever believe right about God if we do not think about what we think about God when our life is going wrong? So, let me ask you: how do you think about God when your life is not going the way you hoped it would? Do not casually dismiss this question.

- When your spouse does not change, how do you think about God?
- When your child remains in sin, how do you think about God?
- When your dream does not come true, how do you think about God?
- When your (fill in the blank) does not happen, how do you think about God?

"Naked I came from my mother's womb, and naked shall I return. The LORD gave, and the LORD has taken away; blessed be the name of the LORD. In all this Job did not sin or charge God with wrong" (Job 1:21–22).

If you cannot come to where Job was in chapter one, you will complicate the misery you are experiencing. It is true that Job began to come unhooked from this stellar response to God, but it does not change what a stellar reaction should be.

I do not have an answer for the suffering you are experiencing. There is an element of mystery to suffering that is a grade level higher than what I understand. Still, yet, there are four things I do know when it comes to personal pain. How you engage and apply these things to your life will proportionally impact how you persevere through suffering.

1. **Formula** – You must not connect your suffering to a formula. The "I do good, and good will happen to me, and if I do bad, then bad things will happen to me" is awful theology.

2. **Mystery** – The Lord loves you beyond your ability to understand His love for you entirely. His intentions toward you are perfect, loving, just, and unassailable.

3. **Sovereignty** – The Lord can do what He pleases, when He wants, how He pleases, for any reason that He wishes, and He is always right.

4. **Worship** – Everything in life should move you into a deeper worship experience with the Lord.

Call to Action

As you reflect upon and pray about those four statements, take some time to journal or talk to a friend about anything that hinders you from fully living out those truths.

If you cannot embrace those truths, there is something about how you think about and relate to the Lord that is not correct. Loving the Lord does not mean getting everything you want or losing any specific thing you possess. Loving the Lord should mean loving the Lord regardless.

1. Can you love the Lord regardless of what you are not receiving from Him?

2. Can you rest in the mystery of His will (Deuteronomy 29:29)?

3. Can you be energized by His grace, while being released from serving a formulaic God?

4. What is it that you want that hinders you from fully realizing this kind of experience with the Lord? That thing, whatever it may be, could be your idol.

Chapter 2

It Makes No Sense

The number one relationship in your life is God, so what you think about Him is the most important thing that should take up your brain space. There are no thoughts higher than our transcendent, infinite, all-powerful God. He is your most effective help when trouble comes into your life (Psalm 46:1), but if your thoughts about Him are insufficient, the assistance you receive from Him will be inadequate.

This truth makes assessing your "God thoughts" one of the most important things you can do. The good news is you can determine your thoughts about God at any time. All you need is one key ingredient. That's personal suffering. Too often the first response to trouble is how to get out of it. That is a mistake. God is in your problem, whatever your issue may be. Your first response should be to discern the mind of God. Just maybe your trouble is the passageway to a more profound experience with God and a better life with others.

Blessed Trouble

The Lord taught me this lesson many years ago after someone murdered my first brother in 1987. After receiving the news of his death, I asked the Lord what He was doing and how did He want me to respond to what was happening. His death did not make sense to me.

That tragedy went beyond my scope of understanding. I needed someone who knew more and could do more to help walk me through that horrible unchangeable situation.

Seeking God did not change my trouble. It did not take away what I had to endure. But it did make all the difference in how I processed the pain. Either I was going to be problem-centered or God-centered during that difficult time.

- The God-centered person shows trust, faith, courage, grace, hope, peace, strength, and clarity when trouble comes.
- The problem-centered person shows fear, worry, anger, despair, vulnerability, and confusion when trouble comes.

It is not that the God-centered person avoids the temptation to worry about or control the situation. Not at all. He may fear episodically or seek to control the situation, but he is mostly managed by faith in God rather than by the tragic circumstances.

- Think about your last difficult season. Were you mostly God-centered or problem-centered?
- Perhaps you are currently in a difficult season. Where do you land on the "God-centered to problem-centered" spectrum?

This problem is what makes Job's response to trouble so amazing (Job 1:20–22). His first response to his disappointment was to worship the Lord. It was only after his counselors came to counsel him that things went from bad to worse.

I am not saying his counselors made things worse, though it appears they did. I would say the Lord used their awful counsel to dig a little deeper into Job's theology. And that was a good thing because

Job's thoughts about God needed to improve. To some degree, Job believed in the retributive principle: if you do good, the Lord will reward you, and if you do bad, the Lord will bring bad into your life. You see the first instance of this in Job 1:5. You also see it interspersed throughout his dialogue with his three friends (Job 3:25).

Job had great thoughts about God, but they were not pure thoughts. He tried hard to avoid adverse outcomes (Job 1:5). He loved the Lord, but he had an unhealthy view of the Lord. Job lived with a low-level fear of the negative (Job 3:25) rather than high-level trust in the Lord. His suffering brought his underdeveloped theology to the surface. Though his friends were a pain in his side, they were also a means of grace, used by the Lord to lay out his entire under-developed theological substructure.

Karma Christians

Maybe you have heard someone say, "I tried Christianity, and it did not work for me." Typically, this kind of statement reveals the retributive principle of doing good, receiving good or doing bad, receiving bad. Life had not gone the way the person hoped, so they tried religion. It is the idea of the plane going down, and everybody becomes religious. In such cases, the Lord becomes the rescuer. The person attempts to manipulate the Lord to get what he wants.

He tries Christianity to achieve a good outcome. This kind of cynicism always ends with disappointment. The Lord is not your insurance agent—at least not that way. You were not made to have all of your dreams fulfilled. You were made to glorify God. Your Creator is the One who determines how you are to live. It is fallenness that distorts your thoughts about God and life.

The temptation is to reduce God to self-serving formulas. You hear it in our language: what goes around, comes around. In a sense, all of us are karma Christians. Don't you feel the tug in your soul:

"If I do well, the Lord will shine His face on me, or if I choose to sin, the Lord will get me."

It is true that there is a law of sowing and reaping (Galatians 6:7). If you put a small metal object in a power outlet, you will be shocked. Your instructor will punish you if you get caught cheating on a test. If you choose to eat anything you want, while not exercising, the chances of having unresolvable health problems are assured.

Sowing and reaping are laws that work some of the time but not all of the time. How many times have you done something dumb and nothing terrible happened to you? When I think about the stupidity of my life, I am amazed at God's grace (Ephesians 2:8–9). I have not, in every way, received everything I deserved. What went around for me did not always come back around to me, and I praise God for this.

Your theology of suffering and sin must come under better theological scrutiny. There are three ways to view the hardship that comes into your life. As I lay them out, which one most accurately describes you?

- **Retributive** – If you do good, things will be okay, but if you do bad, bad things will happen to you (Job 1:5).
- **Presumptuous** – You can sin and get away with it because the Lord is gracious, and you do not live under the law (Psalm 19:13).

- **Trusting** – You have been called to suffer, and sometimes the Lord will use personal suffering to bring about good things in your life (Romans 8:28; 1 Peter 2:21–25).

Radical God

If life worked according to the "do bad, get bad" formula, all you have to do is figure out what you have done wrong and start doing good. This idea is a major tenet of the health-and-wealth gospel.

This kind of theology places power and justice in your hands. It is karma Christianity. It is legalism. Your works are what matter most. It is putting you in the center of the universe while God becomes your divine Santa. You cannot reduce the Lord God Almighty to a formula. You do not serve a manipulatable Lord. Meeting all of your desires and giving you everything you want is not at the top of His to-do list.

To get all of your desires met by the Lord is as unwise as it is unbiblical. No loving parent would parent that way. Getting everything you want is how you become Satan, not Christ (Luke 22:42). The Lord is mysterious (Deuteronomy 29:29). He is not like you (Isaiah 55:8–9); therefore, it is imperative that you understand Him according to who He is, especially during your darkest trials. Here are three critical considerations to factor into your theology of suffering.

1. There are no pat answers.
2. There is an element of mystery in your suffering.
3. God is more significant than what is happening to you.

No Pat Answers

You must factor what the Lord thinks about you and your trouble into your seasons of heartbreak. His answers will always be somewhat different from what others will tell you. This reality is why you must guard against pat answers when life is going sideways. You do not serve a formulaic Lord. There can be times of joy and times of sadness while you should not tie either one of those seasons to your behavior. Sometimes it would be better for you to spend more time with God than with a counselor.

If you go to a counselor, you will receive answers. If you go to the Lord, you may not receive solutions. Job would have been better off if he had not sought the counsel of friends, choosing instead to ask the Lord.

An Element of Mystery

Everything does not have to have an immediate answer. When God does not act like you think He should, it just means He is working in ways you do not yet understand. Your faith is supposed to be in the Lord, not in being omniscient—knowing all the answers. The former will strengthen you in the Lord while the latter will weaken you through self-reliant contrivances.

This perspective means your starting point about God must have goodness built into it. If you do not believe the Lord is good and is seeking your well-being, you will try to take control of your situation by turning your life circumstance into your version of good. This reaction will end with personal disappointment and relational dysfunction.

The Greatness of God

Humans are tempted to give pat answers to unravel the mysteries of life. Sometimes these attempts to figure things out sound hollow when compared to the greatness of God. People still die of debilitating diseases through no fault of their own, and good things happen to bad people.

You live in a world that is out of your control, though it is not out of the Lord's authority. Because of the turned upside down world in which you live, three things will always happen until Jesus comes to straighten out what is crooked.

- The Lord will allow bad things to happen to all people.
- The Lord is in control of all things.
- The Lord is always working for the good of those who trust Him.

How you think about these truths will cause one of two outcomes. Either your circumstances will rule your life as you continuously fight to seize control of what you cannot control, or you will struggle to find rest in the Lord while living in a fallen world (Hebrews 4:11).

Call to Action

What master are you going to serve (Matthew 6:21, 24)? Are you more controlled by your circumstances or by the Lord? If you are seeking to rewrite the script of your life by seizing control of it, you have made yourself a god, which places you in more significant conflict with the Lord than with your problems (James 4:6).

"You gotta serve somebody." —Bob Dylan

If you believe God is good and He is working good in your life, you will be able to find rest in your storms (Matthew 8:24). Who are you going to serve?

- What you think about God is the most important thing you can think.
- The most effective way to discern your thoughts of God is how you respond to your suffering.

If you are genuinely interested in exploring this further, I appeal to you to make these ideas a topic of conversation among your friends. Job had three friends, but they were not the best kind of friends to walk him through his troubles. Yet God was in control of the situation, and He used Job's friends to unpack a weakness in his theology. Will you trust the Lord by bringing your thoughts about God, as understood through your suffering, to your community?

Chapter 3

Blindsided While Doing Good

Say what you want about Job, but he was a good guy. He was a terrific guy who loved God with all his heart, soul, mind, and strength (Matthew 22:37). Listen to the description from the book titled after him:

"There was a man in the land of Uz whose name was Job, and that man was blameless and upright, one who feared God and turned away from evil" (Job 1:1).

I know, I know: there are no good people. I understand. But Job was a guy who tried to do the right thing. I am sure his sin struggles were more episodic than they were patterns. Every now and again he did wrong, but, for the most part, he did well.

Everyone sins. We probably sin daily. But being characterized by sin is not how things ought to be, and Job was not that way. He was a man who loved God. He was a saint who occasionally sinned. He went about doing good. He had a biblically appropriate awareness about the importance of honoring the Lord (Job 1:5). And he was not fearful in his service for the Lord.

Job was faithful, sober-minded, and humble. God blessed him in profound and bountiful ways. And, as you know, his obedience did not automatically give him a free pass from trouble.

There is a trap when you think that if you do good, God will bless or, even worse, that God must bless because you have done the right things. Occasionally, you will hear it stated or implied this way:

"He was a good guy. I don't know why that happened to him. Of all the people to have something terrible to happen to them, I would have never thought it would have been him."

It is a mistake to think when you do good, God must reward you with blessings that fit your preferences. This kind of thinking will not only have an awful impact on your motives, but it will run your thinking off sound theological tracks.

It is a set-up for anger and bitterness toward God. It can create jealousy in the heart as the hurting soul thinks about others who are not suffering as much. In some situations, it will motivate a person to walk away from God. This latter outcome was the insinuation of the devil: Job only served God because God blessed him (Job 1:9). How about you? What are your motives? Do you serve God for something? For nothing? For self? For His glory?

When Turned Upside Down

Job was not allowed to know at the moment of his adversity that what he was receiving was from the hand of the Lord, though later he may have reflected on it as the blast of God (Job 4:9). Though his troubles were a mystery to him, the fire from God did fall, and the winds from His breath did blow, and in a matter of minutes Job's sacred and satisfied life was destroyed (Job 1:20–22).

I think at times there is a desire on our part to protect God's reputation, especially in moments of deep trials. This reaction does not help God, us, or others. We must be honest with His Word: God blindsided Job while he was doing good (Job 1:16).

The radicalness of God demands that we understand how He will allow pain and suffering into our lives (John 3:16). Within minutes Job was sitting in the squalor of his brokenness, and everything that used to be was no more.

I think the first thing that would come to my mind in a situation like this would be something along the lines of, "Why Lord?" It would be easy for me to not only question God about what had happened but be tempted to accuse Him.

Job was different from me. His response was stunning. Rather than accusing God, he took the opportunity during his darkest trial to offer praise to the One he loved most of all. Be amazed at what Job said.

"Then Job arose and tore his robe and shaved his head and fell on the ground and worshiped. And he said, Naked I came from my mother's womb, and naked shall I return. The LORD gave, and the LORD has taken away; blessed be the name of the LORD. In all this Job did not sin or charge God with wrong" (Job 1:20–22).

Worship

When Job fell on the ground, he worshiped the Lord. It bears repeating: he worshipped the Lord. This response to God was not the case with me. When my devastation came into my life, I fell on the ground, too. The difference was that I did not worship God in that moment or in the days that followed. I cried and wailed, longing for God to return the things I had lost. Those things were my wife and two small children.

As I began to submerge myself in the Book of Job, my heart was simultaneously stunned and overwhelmed. Convicted and encouraged. Motivated and directed. Job taught me there was a better way—a better object for my worship. Rather than placing my faith in what I lost, the Lord was teaching me to reestablish my faith in Him.

- When unpleasantness comes into your life, what is your response?
- What do the "turnings of your heart" reveal to you after being cast into the throes of disappointment?

I do not ask these things as your critic. I ask them as a student, who has sat where you may be sitting (Ezekiel 3:15; Daniel 3:1–30). What I have learned in the crucible of suffering is that how you answer those questions will reveal what has gripped your heart (Luke 12:34).

There is a true and living God (or god) whom you worship, and you reveal Him (or it) during the dark times in your life. Job did not have a worship disorder—at least not in the beginning of his trial. Though his soul went into a myriad of complexities later on, in the beginning of his crucible, he was clear-headed. Though he was a saint who sins, which his later ordeal reveals, he knew whom he believed (Job 19:25).

Nakedness

"And he said, Naked I came from my mother's womb, and naked shall I return" (Job 1:21).

He immediately acknowledged his dependence on God as he covered the entire spectrum of his life: Job came into the world dependent (naked) upon the Lord, and he knew he would leave this world dependent (naked) upon the Lord.

Whether it was his past, present, or future, Job was self-aware how he was naked and open before God (Hebrews 4:13). He did not shrink back from a God-centered dependency by striving to rely on himself (2 Corinthians 1:8–9).

He was weak and broken but not a fool (2 Corinthians 4:7). To become self-reliant in your darkest hour is similar to speeding down the Interstate blindfolded as your steering wheel comes off in your hand. For me, somewhere between my naked entrance into this world and my yet-to-be naked exit from this world, I became self-sufficient. As a youngster, I learned how to roll over, crawl, walk, talk, feed myself, and fend for myself.

In time, I drifted from a total state of dependency until I no longer needed God. It was a worldview that believed I was something when in reality I was nothing (Galatians 6:3). The fool says in his heart there is no God, and he is doubly a fool to live as though he does not need Him (Psalm 14:1–7). Job did not think this way. He was a God-centered, God-trusting man.

- Do you see the humbling value of God reminding you how you are naked and how you do need Him?
- What would you be like today without the humbling hand of God working in you?

Bless

"Blessed be the name of the Lord" is what Job said. I love this statement. A great way of understanding it is by thinking about what he did not say. Job did not say, "Blessed be the hand of the Lord."

Do you see the difference? It is one of those transformational differences. Job was laser-locked on the right thing. His primary concern was not what the Lord gave him or took away from him. What mattered to Job was God's name, not His gifts.

Typically, when I came home in the afternoons, when my kids were younger, they would run into the garage to greet me. Inevitably, they were curious as to what I brought home for them as they looked to catch a glimpse of a hopeful blessing from the hand of their daddy. Not so with Job. His eye was not on the hand of God but on the name of God.

- Are you more interested in what God will give you or what He may take away from you? Do you typically praise the Lord regardless of what you receive from Him (Job 38:1–3)?

The best way for you to answer those questions is to think about how you respond when you do not get what you want. (I am still growing in this kind of reorientation of the heart, too.) Through the years, my Lord has reminded me of this truth during those moments, and each blessed reminder has nudged me closer to living more like His Son.

Sinless

Just when you think his response could not be any more profound, listen to the final line, right before the curtain of the first chapter brings us to a suspenseful end:

"In all this Job did not sin or charge God with wrong" (Job 1:22).

Incredible! Some people have characterized Job as a whiny person. Let us not go there right now. How about if you hunker down here for a while and reflect upon how he responded to God before he crawled out of the epicenter of his tragedy.

- What is the one thing in your life you think you could not live without today? Name it if you can.
- If your answer is someone or something other than God, you could be only moments away from sinning and charging God foolishly.

When I lost the three dearest people in my life, it took me four years to fully adjust my thinking about God and the redemptive purposes of suffering. The first chapter of Job represents only part of the things the Lord wanted me to see, learn, and apply. It took me two years to process this chapter.

I felt as though I could not press on until I wholly owned what God was saying through my old friend, Job. His response to tragedy seemed to be an unscalable mountain. Mercifully, the Lord buried me in this chapter because He was relentless in His love for me.

The Spirit of God persistently revealed how I could not move on to the end of Job's book with a heart of transformed freedom until I singularly directed my worship to the Lord Jehovah alone. I had a twisted heart. I was a two-master-lover. I wanted the Lord, and I wanted other things too (Matthew 6:24). In time, God restored my heart to Himself, and I began to see Him in previously hidden ways.

Knowing God and experiencing God are two different things. There are a lot of Christians who know Him but only a few who have experienced Him in the way in which Paul longed to know Him (Philippians 3:10).

Most of us intuitively know the radical nature of God, and it scares us. It should. Our God is a terrible God—a person who wanted Job to experience Him beyond the intellectual know-how, and there is only one path for this kind of divine, experiential profundity (John 12:24). Are you ready to suffer? I am not sure if Job was looking for adversity, but he eventually got it.

God blessed him in the beginning and transformed him in the end. My appeal to you is to give careful consideration to the things that blindside you. You do not want to miss the blessing of extraordinary suffering. Eventually, through the crucible of suffering, Job saw what he was supposed to see, and he was set free.

"I had heard of you by the hearing of the ear, but now my eye sees you; therefore I despise myself, and repent in dust and ashes" (Job 42:5–6).

Chapter 4

When Things Were Going Well

God operates with purpose. There is always a plan behind the madness that is in our lives. Our initial and most important job is to adjust our attitudes to theocentric ways so that we can discern and respond appropriately to Him and others.

Read the seven verses below and tell me if you see what I see. What I want you to look for is the sequential logic of the passage. As you read one verse, you should be able to predict what is going to happen next.

For example, verse nine says Jesus came for His baptism. Then it says John baptized Him. That makes sense. He came to His baptism and John baptized Him. Read on. Anticipate the "ways of the Lord" as you progress through the passage. See if the text meets your expectations.

9 "In those days Jesus came from Nazareth of Galilee and was baptized by John in the Jordan.

10 And when he came up out of the water, immediately he saw the heavens opening and the Spirit descending on him like a dove.

11 And a voice came from heaven, "You are my beloved Son; with you I am well pleased."

12 The Spirit immediately drove him out into the wilderness.

13 And he was in the wilderness forty days, being tempted by Satan. And he was with the wild animals, and the angels were ministering to him.

14 Now after John was arrested, Jesus came into Galilee, proclaiming the gospel of God,

15 and saying, "The time is fulfilled, and the kingdom of God is at hand; repent and believe in the gospel" (Mark 1:9–15).

This passage is stunning. It is sobering. It is also scary. The three verses that do not fit into my flow of logic are verses 12–14. I never anticipated Jesus going from experiencing God's pleasure at His baptism ("You are my beloved Son; with you I am well pleased.") to intense suffering ("The Spirit immediately drove him out into the wilderness."). The transition from good to horrific seemed to happen in the blink of an eye.

Jesus had spent thirty years preparing for His big moment on the public stage. He was on the precipice of building His ministry. The Father affirmed Him. John baptized Him. He had made all the right moves. He had favor with God and with people (Luke 2:52). Now it was time for Him to swing into gospel action.

1. He had come of age.
2. John baptized Him.

54

3. The dove came down.

4. The Father broadcast His favor.

5. He came up from the water.

The next thing you would expect in the flow of thought would be for Jesus to step out of the water, stand on the banks of the Jordan, and tell everyone about how the kingdom of God was at hand (Mark 1:15).

This intersection is where the Spirit of God threw me a curveball. He interrupted my thought process. He caught me off guard. Preaching the kingdom of God was not the next thing on the Father's calendar of events. The next thing was personal suffering. There is an echo of Job in this passage. (See Job 1:13–22.)

A Drive on the Wild Side

The text says the Spirit of God drove Jesus into the wilderness where Satan tempted Him for forty days. There were also wild beasts in the mix along with ministering angels. It's an unexpected and unfathomable scene.

"But he is unchangeable, and who can turn him back? What he desires, that he does. For he will complete what he appoints for me, and many such things are in his mind. Therefore I am terrified at his presence; when I consider, I am in dread of him" (Job 23:13–15).

The first time I saw this passage in this way, I was dumbfounded. It made me afraid. What was the point? Jesus seemingly had done everything He needed to do to be prepared to fulfill the will of His Father. Just when you thought it was safe, things turned dark and dangerous. Isn't this how it goes for most of us? We believe we are okay. We believe we are ready for "come what may." We even assume we know how things should move forward for us.

- The newlyweds expect to live happily ever after.

- The new convert expects all things to work together for good.

- The wife expects her husband to love her well.

- The husband expects his wife to respect him.

- The children expect their parents to represent Christ honorably.

- The healthy person expects a few more years of good living.

Then God throws us a curveball. We find ourselves not enjoying what we expected while toiling under the burden of unforeseen challenges. These kinds of surprises can be devastating and discomfiting to the person with a limited view of God's sovereignty and an inaccurate understanding of the theology of suffering.

"And when he got into the boat, his disciples followed him. And behold, there arose a great storm on the sea, so that the boat was being swamped by the waves" (Matthew 8:23–24).

Just when you thought the sailing would be smooth, the Father throws turbulence your way (Jonah 1:4). While I don't want to make you suspicious or paranoid every time you hear the wind blowing, I think it would be wise for all of us to grapple well with the mysteries of God (Deuteronomy 29:29).

Nobody knows us as God does, and nobody knows what we need like Him (Hebrews 4:13). If the Father was to leave us to our preferences, there is no question we would miss out on some of the most essential and satisfying blessings of life.

Our inherent desire is to avert the steep seasons of our lives. I understand this perspective. Who's looking for trouble? Even though there is an equipping element to the suffering that is essential if any of us are going to be used by the Lord.

Though we should not ask for suffering or live our lives under a cloud of paranoia, it would serve us well to have a biblical perspective on personal pain. Changes, challenges, and hardships are not an anomaly in the Lord's worldview (1 Peter 4:12). Suffering is a gift (Philippians 1:29), a promise (John 16:33), and a calling (1 Peter 2:21) from God.

Many Sides of Love

Have you ever heard the expression, "Just when things were going well, the other shoe fell?" Its meaning conveys the idea of having your life the way you want it, and then suddenly, from out of nowhere, your life goes awry. Like Goldilocks finding the perfect bed, only to be awakened and alarmed by a family of bears.

Some people live in a pessimistic worldview—a form of paranoia, accompanied by a morbid expectancy that God is out to get them. It's a freedom-sapping mindset that marginalizes the power of the gospel in anyone's life (Galatians 5:1, 13). In the Savior's most famous sermon, He told us what to expect from His Father.

"Or which one of you, if his son asks him for bread, will give him a stone? Or if he asks for a fish, will give him a serpent? If you then, who are evil, know how to give good gifts to your children, how much more will your Father who is in heaven give good things to those who ask him!" (Matthew 7:9–11).

The conclusion we should draw from this passage is that if there is trouble in our lives, we should find assurance that the Lord is there and that He is writing something good into our stories. It is upon us to trust Him while responding biblically to the crucible of suffering.

Purposeful God

Personal suffering is one of the most oft-used means the Lord implements to accomplish His useful purposes in our lives. You see one of the most profound illustrations of this in the suffering Savior (Hebrews 4:15).

Sovereign Lord was not only in the suffering of Jesus, but He caused it (Isaiah 53:10). As the pain escalated in the garden of Gethsemane, Jesus asked for a way out of it (Luke 22:42), though He quickly submitted Himself to the shaping of His Father's hammer.

It is possible you did not anticipate the trouble you are experiencing. God did. He ordained it because of the need to fulfill His plans for you. One of the most effective and profound lessons you'll ever learn in life is how to steward the suffering God permits in your life.

To fall short of this wisdom is never to realize all that God could do through you. The person who misses this essential and transformative lesson will grow in their hearts a garden of bitter herbs. The humble and pliable soul will be broken by the suffering as they are learning to rejoice in the darkness. Their pain will begin to reshape them into rejoicing lights that radiate the glory of God (2 Corinthians 12:9).

Blessed by Weakness

The passage in Mark says some angels ministered to Jesus while He was suffering in the desert (Mark 1:13). There is a glorious paradox here: God ministers to those in need—a core tenet of the gospel: God helps the needy.

"And when Jesus heard it, he said to them, Those who are well have no need of a physician, but those who are sick. I came not to call the righteous, but sinners" (Mark 2:17).

I think if most of us were honest, we would prefer not to suffer, which means we would be willing to forego a rich experience with the Lord that can only come through disappointment and challenges. But therein lies the problem: we despise being weak. One of our greatest fears is finding ourselves in the position of not being able to extricate ourselves from our difficulties.

When we find ourselves in that place, the most important thing for us to do is experience God at the moment. How are you experiencing God in your suffering? What is He teaching you? How is He ministering to you? How are you changing? Trying to escape your problems may seem wise, but discerning the Lord's plans for you is wiser.

It is not wrong to try to extricate yourself from your troubles, but it is wrong to miss the Lord's purposes for your problems. The path to being redemptive in the lives of others is a path of suffering. As Christ was beginning His public ministry, the Spirit of God drove Him into the wilderness for essential testing.

The tested man or woman, who has been transformed by the Lord through the testing, is the most qualified person to be redemptive in the lives of others. Suffering is the path that leads to public ministry and your greatest usefulness to God and others. The people in the Bible that God used the most were those who suffered the most.

People whose first response is to get out of their trouble do not understand or accept the necessity of experiencing the Lord in the crucible of suffering. Though their chief aim is to save their lives, the result of their actions may lead them to "losing" their lives.

"If anyone would come after me, let him deny himself and take up his cross and follow me. For whoever would save his life will lose it, but whoever loses his life for my sake and the gospel's will save it." (Mark 8:34–35).

Shalom Acquired

There is a peace that passes all understanding (Philippians 4:7), but it comes with a condition: you have to die to yourself. Nothing will challenge you more or let you know where you stand with the Lord and others than how you respond to your trials.

- What are you going through right now?
- How are you responding to your trial?
- Is your heart guarded against the traps of grumbling and bitterness?
- What has the Lord revealed to you about you?
- How do you need to change?

I wish I could make your trouble go away. I cannot. Sometimes our problems are as surprising to us as what happened to Jesus in the early stages of Mark's narrative. We never saw it coming.

Just when everything was going fine, the other shoe fell, and now you're out for the count. Or, are you? Is your trouble drawing you closer to the Lord? If not, will you share these things with a close friend?

Chapter 5

When God Does Not Come Through

Shari took a shortcut to work. After arriving on the company campus, she learned of an accident on her usual route. A tractor-trailer overturned. No one was hurt, but it stopped the traffic for three hours. She thanked God for directing her differently that morning.

Jared received an unexpected check in the mail for $3,500. It was an IRS oversight. Jared was sharing with his small group how he and Jennie had prayed, asking the Lord to provide for a recent medical emergency. God came through for them.

William and Caroline just came home from a fantastic honeymoon. With stars in her eyes, Caroline floated into work the following Monday. The Lord gave her exactly what she wanted: the man of her dreams.

All three of these stories have two things in common: their desires were met, and they were satisfied with the outcomes. They were happy because they received what they wanted. The Lord was kind to them. I have been thinking about this idea of being onboard with God when positive outcomes happen while being distraught or angry about results that do not meet my expectations.

The classic passage for this line of thinking is Job 1:21. I am talking about Job's response to the adverse outcomes that came into his life. Job did not receive what he wanted, but his response to disappointment was astounding, as well as convicting.

"And he said, 'Naked I came from my mother's womb, and naked shall I return. The LORD gave, and the LORD has taken away; blessed be the name of the LORD'" (Job 1:21).

I remember the first time I read this passage. It was profound then, and it is still world-shaking. Job was experiencing an outcome that was the farthest thing from his expectations.

After he surveyed the scene and processed the data, he began to praise God for the good and the bad that came into his life. Say what you will about Job, but in this passage, at this moment, he got it right. Job's astounding response to disappointment has never left me. God has used it mostly in the disappointing times in my life.

- Job's response has been God's healing when the news came about the deaths of my two brothers.
- Job's response has been God's admonition when sitting at a traffic light that had interrupted my life.
- Job's response has been God's appeal when my wife and I were not getting along.
- Job's response has been God's hope when I was out of work with no opportunities forthcoming.

I typically do not have a problem thanking God when I get what I want. It is when I cannot muster praise to God for the difficulties in my life that you would be correct to assume that my gratitude for the good things is more about me than God. If all I can do is praise God for good outcomes, I have laced my praise with a lot of self-focus and self-expectation.

Mature Christianity is when a person can see God working through the hardships while not being overcome by those difficulties. It is further exemplified by genuine worship to God for the high privilege to walk in the steps of His dear Son.

"For to this, you have been called, because Christ also suffered for you, leaving you an example, so that you might follow in his steps" (1 Peter 1:21).

Disappointment is how I usually think when I am being interrupted by the traffic lights of life. I do not have to ask the Lord to give me feedback on my sanctification. I do not have to ask a friend how I am doing. All I have to do is measure my immediate, knee-jerk response to the traffic lights and busy intersections that come into my life.

At the moment of not getting my way, the response that comes from my heart is the most accurate and most objective measurement of my authentic Christian faith. Job was not perfect, as we learn from the succeeding chapters, but he also was not a Christian rookie. Job was a mature Christian, who was not entirely sanctified. Though I would love to experience what Job did at the end of the book (Job 42:10), it would be satisfying enough for me to possess what he had at the beginning of the book.

"There was a man in the land of Uz whose name was Job, and that man was blameless and upright, one who feared God and turned away from evil" (Job 1:1).

Wouldn't you like to have what Job had? To regularly turn away from evil, choosing God instead, is a compelling testimony. If you want to get to this place in your daily walk with the Lord, there are at least two things you have to do.

Good Suffering?

You must broaden your definition of the word good and improve your weak view of suffering. Having your mind changed about these two things could revolutionize your life. Typically, we understand good to be along the lines of health, wealth, and satisfying relationships. Meaning, we want what we want. This perspective is a cultural-centric worldview, not the Bible's view of how things are in a cursed world.

People have a hard time budgeting difficulty, suffering, and frustration into their lives. While I understand the desire to stay away from adverse outcomes, it is myopic to try to orchestrate your life according to your preferences.

It is also a prescription that will lead to bitterness, unforgiveness, cynicism, and broken relationships. Good and suffering can be synonyms in the Bible. They are similar to the word gospel, which we call good news. The problem is how some people do not pull the curtain back far enough to see how the good news became the good news. The gospel is as much about death as it is about a resurrection.

"For it has been granted to you that for the sake of Christ you should not only believe in him but also suffer for his sake" (Philippians 1:29).

Good Christian folks do not want to talk like this. Suffering is considered the unmentionable side of Christianity, rather than a necessary component for the Christian life. Personal pain is one of the most significant ways you can relate to Christ.

It most assuredly is one of the most potent ways He relates to you (Hebrews 4:15). Why can't we reverse the tables and see the benefits and possibilities of suffering? To miss this point is to miss out on your best life now.

1. Is your view of good more like the three stories at the beginning of this chapter?
2. Have you trained yourself to hunt for the benefits that are in the difficulties in your life?
3. What is your knee-jerk response to disappointment?
4. What does your response say about your practical theology?

Living in a Parallel World

Job lived biblically in a parallel world. On the ground level, he was a man of sorrows who was acquainted with grief (Isaiah 53:3). From a sovereignty of God level, he was secure and worshipful (James 1:5–8). He had a high view of God, which was more controlling than his difficulties on the ground. Regardless of the adverse outcomes in his life, his perspective and understanding of the Lord were what kept him stable (Job 19:25).

We all live in a parallel universe. On the ground, we engage thorns and thistles (Genesis 3:18). You are pricked daily with disappointment. All of the paths in your life have the mark of evil on them.

This reality was Joseph's testimony. He was willing to recognize and acknowledge the evil that came into his life (Genesis 50:20). He did not sugarcoat his problems. He called it for what it was rather than ignoring the obvious. Like Job, he did not fixate on the bad things that had happened to him. He lived in the parallel. He recognized the evil, but he filtered it through the sovereignty of God.

Joseph firmly believed that God was in his mess. No matter how powerful or disappointing his life was unfolding, he knew that nothing would shake him down to the ground to where fear, anger, regret, or bitterness were his all-controlling heart issues.

"For I am sure that neither death nor life, nor angels nor rulers, nor things present nor things to come, nor powers, nor height nor depth, nor anything else in all creation, will be able to separate us from the love of God in Christ Jesus our Lord" (Romans 8:38–39).

From Bad to Worse

Embracing good suffering is one of the biggest struggles in the Christian community today. No matter how much we give assent to affirming this truth, when the rubber meets the road, most Christians respond sinfully to their disappointments. Humbly embracing this reality is a vast, life-altering, worldview-shaping deal.

Let me put it this way: if you cannot get this right, your life will muddle along in low-grade disappointments because of your unwillingness to give God space and time to mature you through the crucible of suffering. The best news of the gospel does not come until after the bad news. If we will not learn about God in the bad news, we will never be able to experience satisfaction in the good news.

"And going a little farther he fell on his face and prayed, saying, 'My Father, if it be possible, let this cup pass from me; nevertheless, not as I will, but as you will'" (Matthew 26:39).

When a person does not biblically process the suffering in their lives, several sin patterns will begin to accrue in their minds. If they regularly give way to these trends, they will grow into a self-defeated life. Let me illustrate with the common problem of disappointment. When something terrible happens to us, typically the first thing we experience is disappointment. This response should be a signal that turns us to God, but all too often that is not the case. If we do not turn to the Lord, we will enter into a progression that can look like the following:

- **Regret (or Refusal)** – Rather than turning to God, we begin to think about would've, should've, could've—the things we ought to do differently to gain a more preferred outcome.

- **Bitterness** – If the disappointment stays and we cannot change our circumstances to gain a more preferred outcome, bitterness will soon take root in our souls. We can become distant, critical, numb, fearful, and angry.

- **Unforgiveness** – Rather than looking to God to figure out what He is up to in our situations, we begin to find others to blame. Once we are locked in on the targets, these people become the reasons our lives are not the way they're supposed to be.

- **Self-Righteousness** – A greater than/better than attitude always accompanies unforgiveness. You cannot look down on another person and punish them for what is wrong in your life without being superior to them (Matthew 18:33).

- **Relational Dysfunction** – As you can imagine, a person like this barrels toward relational dysfunction. At this point, it will be hard for them to see how the problem is more about their relationship with God than their relationship with another human.

- **More Poor Choices** – From here, they make more poor choices. Out of a heart of frustration, due to the accumulative effect of the responses already mentioned, the person is tempted to choose more poor responses.

Do you see yourself anywhere on this list? Before you move on, let me appeal to you to work through the call to action at the end of this chapter. Pray through the questions. Ask the Lord to make Job's response your response:

"The LORD gave, and the LORD has taken away; blessed be the name of the LORD" (Job 1:21b).

Call to Action

1. How has your definition of good changed by reading this chapter?
2. In what ways have you experienced the goodness of God through your trials?
3. List at least two ways you need to change your response when unfavorable circumstances come into your life.

Chapter 6

An Unchanging Situation

What would you rather have if you only had one choice: a change of circumstances or a change of mind about your conditions? This question is critical, as well as tied directly to the quality of life you will experience with God and others.

I suspect most of us would prefer a change of circumstances over a change of mind about our situations. The unintended consequence of this perspective is perpetual vulnerability to your circumstances. It is a formula for being controlled by your conditions rather than having victory over them.

The only way to live victoriously, according to this worldview, is always to have favorable circumstances, which is an unrealistic probability. Think about the last negative thing that happened to you. How did you respond? That response is vital in showing you what you cherish the most (Matthew 6:21).

1. A wrong response is a controlling demand for your circumstances to change.

2. A grace-empowered response is an acknowledgment that Sovereign Lord is in control.

Valuing Losses

Mable wants her husband to change. She is right. He should repent. Sin has captured him, and for several reasons he has not been able to extricate himself from his caught-ness (Galatians 6:1). She has become frustrated and impatient with him. Rather than helping her husband through his sin, she is complicating the problem by being demanding, controlling, and critical.

Biff has a wayward child, and he has not tried to hide his displeasure with his son. Like Mable, he has a good desire, but the rebellion has tempted him to sin. The Lord is too slow for Biff. He wants his son to change today, and he is resorting to all kinds of sinful actions to reel his wayward child back into the fold (Matthew 18:12).

What Mable and Biff don't know is that God is more interested in helping them change their minds than their circumstances. When Job reflected upon his seemingly unchangeable circumstances, he fell to the ground and offered a worship-filled response to his Lord. His reflections were more on the Lord of his situation than the horrible events in his life.

"Naked I came from my mother's womb, and naked shall I return. The LORD gave, and the LORD has taken away; blessed be the name of the LORD" (Job 1:21).

If your goal is for your situation to change, which is not a bad goal, the first step in that process is how you think about what is happening to you. We miss this point so quickly when staring trouble in the face.

Job seemed to perceive how his gains and losses were not as significant as the God who was in the gains and losses. The New Testament equivalent to this kind of God-centered thinking was Paul.

"But whatever gain I had, I counted as loss for the sake of Christ" (Philippians 3:7).

Paul learned how to live counter to his world (Philippians 4:11–13). He was not impressed with the things his culture offered. For him, reputation, image, position, power, materialism, affluence, relevance, style, or any other thing that would give him bragging rights were comparable to manure.

He took all the good things that he possessed and threw them in the garbage heap because he found something that surpassed those human-made aspirations. He moved his good accomplishments from the gain column to the loss column, which left nothing in his gain column but Christ.

- Jesus + Nothing = Salvation
- Jesus + Nothing = Sanctification

You are at your strongest when the surpassing worth of knowing Christ causes all other loves in your life to fade in the background. Authentic Christianity is relinquishing all of your desires from rulership in your heart for the opportunity to gain Christ.

"Now great crowds accompanied him, and he turned and said to them, 'If anyone comes to me and does not hate his own father and mother and wife and children and brothers and sisters, yes, and even his own life, he cannot be my disciple. Whoever does not bear his own cross and come after me cannot be my disciple'" (Luke 14:25–27).

You should not attempt to add Jesus to the plus column of your life along with everything else that you want. To have Jesus plus other things will always leave you vulnerable to those other things. This unbiblical cluster will create an unnecessary competition in your heart. You will forever live in tension until Christ rules supreme in your mind.

That I Might Know Him

Though Paul was a great man who accomplished many things that surpassed nearly everyone else of his day, he was willing to let go of all those things because he found something that was superior. Will you do this?

Paul had a change of mind about those perceived good things in his life. He began to see how the things he cherished could be overvalued even to the point of controlling him. He learned how there was only one thing that needed to reign supreme in his heart (Matthew 6:24).

This lesson is one of the hardest things for any person to learn. To be willing to let go of everything you value for the sake of Christ is the ultimate victory and your most significant challenge, which is why many people chose not to follow Jesus any longer (Matthew 19:22).

Are you willing to count everything in life as a minus for the sake of Christ? I'm not asking you to walk away from all of the things you possess. This appeal is not a call for self-flagellation or a vow to poverty so that you can prove that Christ is most important.

I'm asking you if you could be okay if Christ were all you had. If your world falls apart and all the advantages you once had are no longer yours to have, can you get to the place in your thinking where knowing Christ is enough?

God is not calling you to punish yourself by ascetic practices. He is not a mean parent who wants to harm you by taking things away from you. Some people live with this view, always thinking the other shoe is going to fall because God does not want to bless them.

This kind of thinking is foolish. The Father gave His Son to die on the cross for you. If someone gave up his child so you could live, I think it would be safe to say that you are loved, and He would not withhold any good thing from you. (See John 15:13, 3:16; Psalm 84:11.)

His desire is not to withhold but to release you from the captivation and domination that things can have over your thinking, even if those things are your closest relationships. He knows the only way to be strong is by being willing to suffer the loss of all things while standing in the confidence of Christ's faithfulness on your behalf.

You are not strong because you can control your universe. Your strength is proportional to the degree in which you're resting in Christ's ability. Paul knew this, and when he looked at his foundation, he realized he had built it with the wood, hay, and straw of personal accomplishments (1 Corinthians 3:12).

His rank, pedigree, standing, and influence became rubbish in his mind because he knew those things were manufactured and maintained by his strength. He let those things go knowing there was something better found in Christ (Philippians 3:10).

You are only as strong as your vulnerabilities. Paul decided to chuck anything that made him weak, which was everything the world called strong (1 Corinthians 1:18–25). He made the great exchange: I will replace all my worth with the surpassing worth of knowing Jesus.

He learned the secret to life: for when I am weak, I am strong (2 Corinthians 12:10), which brings you to a penetrative question: where are you vulnerable? What is the one thing you don't want to lose? Job said it this way,

"For the thing that I fear comes upon me, and what I dread befalls me. I am not at ease, nor am I quiet; I have no rest, but trouble comes" (Job 3:25–26).

What is the one thing you pray God won't take from you? Be careful here. God is not that mean parent who wants to watch you suffer. He wants to bless you. God gave you His Son. The next biggest blessing He could ever give you is to free you from being controlled by things.

Steps to Freedom

If you are controlled by what you are afraid of losing, you need to be free. You must mentally let those things go so that they no longer dominate you. You must be "okay" with losing all things while obtaining Christ as your most valued treasure.

"He considered the reproach of Christ greater wealth than the treasures of Egypt, for he was looking to the reward" (Hebrews 11:26).

You will never be free until you are willing to forsake all things for the sake of Christ. Do you remember when you renounced the world for the greater riches found in Christ at salvation? Now it is time to forsake the world for those greater riches found in Christ during your sanctification.

Step One – The first step to freedom is to realize the nature of the call on your life. The Lord is systematically and incrementally putting you to death (Romans 12:1–2). The more you resist death, the more difficult you will make your life and your relationships (John 12:24).

Step Two – The second step to access the surpassing worth of knowing Christ is to identify those things that mean the most to you. These are the things that control you. If you don't know what these things are, think about your fears or your anger.

Fear or anger are the typical responses from the person who is losing something they don't want to miss. You must name it and claim it. You have to own your sin. Your mind must be renewed and released from these things. If you're not willing to name what competes for your heart treasure, you will never change.

* What situation in your life tempts you to anger?
* What situation in your life tempts you to fear?
* What person in your life are you trying to control?
* What situation are you trying to bend to conform to what you want?

Step Three – The third step is to confess these things. Paul admitted that he enjoyed what he had and what he was in his former life. There was a long time in his life where he was not going to let go of those things. Like Gollum from "The Lord of the Rings," who loved his gold ring, what Paul possessed was his "precious."

Those things altered his thinking to the point of ruling his life. Part of Paul's process of being released from this bondage was to let others know what those things were and how they dominated his thinking. He made a public confession (Philippians 3:3–6).

One of the most freeing things you can do is articulate what has gripped your mind. Let others in on your fears. When you look out over the landscape of your life and see people or situations who are not meeting your expectations, how do you respond?

If it is sinful, you have yet to find your surpassing worth in Christ. You are not free (John 8:36), and you will never be free until you do. Carefully read the rest of Paul's public confession and ask the Father to help you to emulate his example.

"But whatever gain I had, I counted as loss for the sake of Christ. Indeed, I count everything as loss because of the surpassing worth of knowing Christ Jesus my Lord. For his sake I have suffered the loss of all things and count them as rubbish, in order that I may gain Christ" (Philippians 3:7–8).

What would you rather have if you only had one choice: a change of circumstances or a change of mind about your circumstances? This question is critical and ties directly to the quality of life you will experience with God and others. I'm not sure if the Lord will ever change your circumstances. I am sure He can change your mind about your circumstances.

Chapter 7

Bringing God Down to Your Level

When the circumstances are the most adverse, the temptation will be the strongest to bring God down to your level so that you can argue with Him. "Letting" God be God is one of our greatest fears.

When unexplained and undeserved suffering comes into your life will you still trust the Lord? When God is silent, and there is no apparent benefit to hold on to Him by faith, will you continue to follow Him? Can a believer lose everything that is dear to him and still have robust, God-centered confidence and great love for God?

To answer these questions in the affirmative requires a high view of God, which means God is God and you are not. The Lord can do what He wants to do, when He wants to do it, how He wants to do it, and what He does is perfect and unassailable.

"When we suffer, it is much easier to lower your view of God than to lift your faith higher." —John Walton

There are some types of suffering where lifting your faith to a high view of God can be the most challenging thing you will ever do. An elevated view of God means He is perfect in every way and everything that He does is right and without argument.

"But he is unchangeable, and who can turn him back? What he desires, that he does. For he will complete what he appoints for me, and many such things are in his mind. Therefore I am terrified at his presence; when I consider, I am in dread of him" (Job 23:13–15).

When you are walking through the valley of the shadow of death (Psalm 23:4), to lift up your faith to a high view of God is not only challenging, but it is scary. It is far easier to bring God down to your human understanding where He can be challenged, corrected, and even disobeyed.

To lift Him up to His throne and to worship Him on His throne requires the kind of submission that may cost your life (Matthew 16:24). A high view of God is a call to let God be God regardless of what comes your way. It is a complete surrender of one's life.

"Father, if you are willing, remove this cup from me. Nevertheless, not my will, but yours, be done" (Luke 22:42).

This relinquishing of your rights is the highest call of humankind: to "let" God be God and to be okay with how He runs the universe. The truth is, God will be God whether you let Him or not. The real issue is whether you will be okay with how He runs the universe— most specifically, how He runs your life.

A God You Can Argue With

"And (Job) said, 'Naked I came from my mother's womb, and naked shall I return. The LORD gave, and the LORD has taken away;

blessed be the name of the LORD.' In all this Job did not sin or charge God with wrong" (Job 1:20–21).

It is rare to have a first response like what Job did when your world blows up in your face. To worship and bless the Lord during acute suffering is not typically something that comes from His creation.

Our first response is usually more along the lines of bringing Him down to our level so that we can challenge Him. A non-Sovereign god is a challenge-able god (Isaiah 55:8–9). If the Lord was not Lord, but more like us, what He brings to our lives would be open for debate.

I remember the first time I argued with God this way. It was when my suffering was beyond my ability to manage it (2 Corinthians 1:8–9). When my pain was not as intense, I was okay with Him being God. I never considered going toe-to-toe with the Lord during the good times.

After my sufferings went beyond the breaking point, my desperation increased, and I began to lose my sense of divine propriety. Rather than responding like Job, I sounded more like Job's wife (Job 2:9).

I did this by unwittingly trying to wrestle His divine attributes away from Him. Rather than Him being sovereign, I wanted to be sovereign. Rather than Him determining what good was, I wanted to be the authority on what was right.

Here is a list of ten of His many attributes. After I humanized Him, I could become the determiner of who would control these attributes.

1. The Solitariness of God – He does not need us.
2. The Decrees of God – His (scary) future purposes.

3. The Knowledge of God – He is omniscient.

4. The Immutability of God – He is unchangeable.

5. The Sovereignty of God – He rules everything.

6. The Holiness of God – He is perfect in every way.

7. The Power of God – He is all-powerful.

8. The Faithfulness of God – He is persevering.

9. The Goodness of God – He is the best.

10. The Love of God – He is kind.

These are only ten of His attributes. There are many more. As you can see, to let God be the sole owner of these qualities is to release yourself to His control fully. This need requires you to elevate your faith beyond your ability to manage your life (2 Corinthians 12:10).

High View of God

"And the LORD said to Satan, 'Behold, all that he has is in your hand. Only against him do not stretch out your hand.' So Satan went out from the presence of the LORD" (Job 1:12).

Typically, people are cool with God until personal suffering comes into their lives. It is when He chooses to let down whatever protective hedge (Job 1:10) He has around us that we become unsettled about who He is and what He may allow into our lives.

This possibility is why it is easier to lower your view of God than to have faith in Him. A lower perspective gives you twisted permission to accuse Him of wrongdoing or unfairness. You could even choose to walk away from Him.

"At the moment when faith is hardest and least likely, that is when faith is needed most." —John Walton

Have you ever lowered your view of God when there was an elevated crisis in your life? Take a look at the attribute list again. Which ones have been the most difficult for you to embrace when your suffering was the acutest? Here are some of the ways I have lowered my view of God during personal suffering and, thus, permitted myself to argue with Him as I have tried to call the shots.

- **The Knowledge of God** – Lord, if you know all things, why have you let this in my life? You knew what was coming (decrees of God), but you allowed it anyway.
- **The Immutability of God** – Lord, you are all-powerful (omnipotence). You can change your mind (decrees). You do not have to let my suffering continue.
- **The Sovereignty of God** – Lord, you rule over the entire universe. It would not take much for you (power) to orchestrate things in such a way to make things better for me.
- **The Love of God** – Lord, do you love me? Is this (goodness) how you express love to your children?

"Oh, that I knew where I might find him, that I might come even to his seat! I would lay my case before him and fill my mouth with arguments" (Job 23:3–4).

As you can see, when the Lord is on my level, I can challenge any number of His attributes. I can also interweave several characteristics into my arguments to make a case against Him.

83

Two Conclusions

"What comes into our minds when we think about God is the most important thing about us." —A. W. Tozer

Your crucible of suffering provides you with your most accurate litmus test to examine what you think about God, others, and life. Do not miss that Job's first response to his suffering (Job 1:20–22) was not to God but to others.

He was letting others know what he thought about God. What do others learn about your faith when suffering comes into your life? You always put your beliefs before others, whatever your faith may be.

In the first chapter of Job, his friends saw a man who trusted God. His suffering revealed his faith. His friends could draw two conclusions about Job's faith in the Lord.

- Nothing ever happens to us that is outside of God's control.
- Job truly believed the Lord gives and He takes away, and you can accept both of these possibilities as coming from Him.

This truth includes all primary and secondary causes, which means suffering that comes from the Lord and suffering that comes from others or other circumstances. All suffering, no matter from where it comes, is allowed by the Lord.

This fact does not mean you have to like what God is allowing in your life. It says you should be able not to choose a wrong path when bad things are happening to you. Your sinfulness or lack of sin during your suffering will reveal the kind of faith you possess.

- As you read Job's response to suffering, how do your typical reactions to pain compare to his?

- How do you need to change? Be specific and practical?

Faith means trusting God when there is no apparent reason to do so. When you see unexplained or undeserved suffering, you can have a higher view of yourself than of God. You can think that your love and your justice is better than God's love and justice.

You can do this with any attribute of God. It can be a natural temptation to sit in judgment of God when life is not going your way. Whenever your heart is acting out of faithlessness, you will seek to take control of the situation, even if it means making accusations against the Lord or hurting those who are interfering with what you are trying to control.

- Which attribute of the Lord brings you the most significant struggle?
- How does this struggle impede what the Lord would like to do for you?

Call to Action

Ultimately, the battle is between faith and fear. When trouble comes, people are afraid. The Lord is always calling you to faith (to trust). The degree of difficulty in trusting the Lord is in proportion to the fear of what you perceive your losses to be.

As you sense something in your life being wrestled away from you, the more you will fight, even if that fight is against God. This reaction is not what Job was willing to do. He was not going to war. He was going to trust. The Lord gave, and the Lord was taking away. He chose to worship God at that moment. If you are not like Job, name the thing you are afraid of losing. It is that thing that is sabotaging your faith.

In the space of twelve months, I lost my wife, children, home, property, job, and reputation. These lost things were easy to identify. I did not want to lose them, but I could not control them, so I became angry with God and others. Maybe the thing you are afraid of losing is less discernible, though I doubt it. Most of us know the something we do not want to lose, and when something challenges it, we can become angry and faithless.

This intersection is where you will have to make a life-altering decision. Will you be honest about the real motives of your heart? If you cannot or will not do this, you will always live a life that will oscillate between anger and fear.

The first step in transcending your trouble is to be honest with what is going on in your heart. Because I did not respond like Job, it took a while for me to be honest with God and others. I had to own my sin by naming my fear. Only then did I begin a process of repenting of this fear of loss, while trusting the Lord.

If you can relate to this chapter, I strongly encourage you not to walk this journey alone. Bring trusted friends into this battle for your soul. The mortification of sin does not happen at a point in time. It is a journey suited for a community.

Chapter 8

When Trouble Comes

Biff was having a good day. He just came from an extended weekend at the beach with his family. Time well spent is how he put it on Monday morning. He was alive, refreshed, and ready to do battle with the business of the week. By Tuesday, our old friend Biff was slumping back into his all too familiar patterns. Rather than being feisty and hope-filled, he sounded more like Elijah squatting under a dead Juniper tree.

"But he himself went a day's journey into the wilderness and came and sat down under a broom tree. And he asked that he might die, saying, 'It is enough; now, O LORD, take away my life, for I am no better than my fathers'" (1 Kings 19:4).

Do you recognize yourself in Elijah? I see myself in our faithful servant (James 5:17). One minute I am kicking Baal booty all over Mount Carmel (1 Kings 18:27), and the next moment I am bemoaning my very existence.

Whenever our circumstances control us too much, we need to reevaluate how we think about and respond to God who is in our situations. Your trouble is one of your prime moments to diagnose the exact condition of your soul. Though there are times I want to think I am better than I am, it is when trouble comes that I know the real truth about my spiritual condition.

Typically, the problem-centered person orbits around a constellation of thoughts and attitudes that vie for control of his soul. Here are a few of the antagonists that seek to captivate the troubled mind.

Decreasing contentment	Growing unrest
Lack of gratitude	Cloudy judgment
Gnawing negativity	Temptation to retreat
Hope deprived	Impoverished motivation
Controlling fear	Relational distance
Weakened faith	

Like a busy intersection, with more cars piling on by the hour, these are a few of the symptoms of the problem-centered soul. Once you begin down this one-way street, there is only one outcome unless you make a substantial course correction.

The most dangerous sign of all is the last one—weakened faith. When troubles hover over us like a dark cloud—and those things control, shape, and define us, we will take a hit, and our lives will begin to deny the transformative power of the gospel.

When Stuff Happens

Paul went through a lot of stuff (2 Corinthians 1:8–9). Sometimes he dipped way down into the difficulties (2 Corinthians 4:7–12) to the point of despair (2 Corinthians 12:7–10). But his problems did not characterize him.

There is a difference between episodic disappointment when trouble comes versus living in a continual cloud of being overwhelmed by your problems until it reshapes how you think about and react to life. Either I am maturing through my difficulties by becoming stronger each day or my soul is regressing as a new wave of trials roll over me. Losing heart or being renewed day by day: these are our two choices.

"So we do not lose heart. Though our outer nature is wasting away, our inner nature is being renewed day by day" (2 Corinthians 4:16).

How about it? Are you problem-centered or God-centered? The God-centered or faith-filled person will not only believe there is no temptation greater than God's empowering grace, but his attitudes, words, and actions will affirm this truth (1 Corinthians 10:13). God's faithfulness to the God-centered person will be the wave he rides through the trials of life (Psalm 42:7). Even in the darkest of nights, he will be able to reorient his mind while regaining a gospel-centered equilibrium properly.

We should be able to successfully live within the antithetical tension of good and evil (Genesis 50:20). Though we are regularly cast down, we can respond in faith toward God, while mustering praise to Him (Psalm 42:11). We do this because our attitudes are shaped and controlled by this powerful truth:

"Little children, you are from God and have overcome them, for he who is in you is greater than he who is in the world" (1 John 4:4).

Functional vs. Intellectual

Perhaps you know these truths to be true. Maybe you can say, "Yes, Rick, I know I should not be controlled by my problems, but for me, the things I know (intellectual theology) do not represent my day-to-day functional theology."

There is always a distance between what we know and how we live, which is true for all of us. Our intellectual theology is more than our functional theology. Knowing truth is one thing: living truth is a whole other matter.

We need a practical plan that will help us process through our problems. We need to know how to think, act, and respond to our troubles. What I want to lay out for you is a simple way to think about your situational challenges. It is a seven-step process that can transform you. To gain the most benefit, I recommend you work through this process in the context of trusted friends.

Step One – Discern the Purpose

There can be many reasons a problem enters your life (Deuteronomy 29:29). You will never fully understand the complete mind of God on why He allows trouble to come to you (Job 1:6–12). Even so, you will find assurance in this: God allows problems to come into your life to help you transform into His Son. Many times your transformation happens because of your suffering.

Typically, when a problem comes into people's lives, the first thing they think about is the other person on the other end of the problem. That is a mistake. It will obscure what the Lord could teach them. I would go so far as to say if you miss this essential step, you will not be able to process the problem at hand successfully. When trouble comes, the first order of business should be to have a personal conversation with God.

Let me illustrate: Biff and Mable have ongoing rough spots in their marriage. Shortly after arriving home one evening, Biff learns that Mable overspent money on clothes. This incident is not the first time she has done this.

Rather than seeking the Lord first—trying to discern how he could learn, grow, and mature through this problem—Biff chose to go off on Mable. Rather than adjusting his heart before the Lord, he tried to fix Mable. Biff made things worse.

Diagnostic Questions: When trouble comes your way, are you quick to judge your heart before you address others who may be part of the problem?

Step Two – Discern Your Heart

It would have been better for Biff to discern how the Lord wanted to change his heart. If your first call is not to place the spiritual stethoscope over your heart so you can carefully judge yourself, you will taint your judgments of others (Matthew 7:3–5).

A more mature believer would have discerned how God was in his trouble. Rather than being an accuser of his spouse, he would have been an expectant seeker, knowing God was up to something good (Romans 8:28).

Diagnostic Questions: When you have addressed your heart first and adjusted yourself accordingly, how did things turn out for you? How about when you did not assess your heart first. How did it go?

Step Three – Discern Hardness

"Today, if you hear his voice, do not harden your hearts" (Hebrews 4:7).

By not addressing what God was seeking to do in Biff first, he began laying down a thin veneer over his heart. This effect will ultimately blind him to his weaknesses and proclivities (1 Timothy 4:2). I have done this too many times in my relationship with Lucia. She may do something that I do not like. I immediately respond in a careless and non-sanctifying way.

Rather than adjusting my heart first and benefiting from the Lord's sanctifying work, I try to change her. When I do this, I miss some of the underlying sins in my heart that drive my responses toward her and, thus, I botch up our relationship even further.

Diagnostic Question: When you think about your conflict, what are some of the more common underlying sins in your heart—things the Spirit of God is providing illumination for you to see regarding yourself?

Step Four – Identify and Isolate

One of the most dangerous places a person can be is not able to hear the Spirit's voice, an inability to discern the trickery of his heart. This spot is no man's land—a place where you can easily exchange the truth of God for a lie because of a desire to press His truth out of your life (Romans 1:18, 25).

Flying blind through life, not able to discern the evil machinations of your heart, is a dance with the devil in the dark.

Diagnostic Questions: What did you write down in response to the previous diagnostic question? Are you able to identify and isolate the sin(s) that seek to capture your heart when trouble comes into your life? Would you be willing to discuss these things with trusted friends —maybe your small group?

Step Five – See What You Can't See

If you jump to the person on the other end of your problem too quickly, while missing how your heart is deceiving you, then you will miss out on the work of God in your life. It is a mercy from the Lord to bring thorns into your life (2 Corinthians 12:7–10). It allows you to see yourself more clearly.

Aren't we so easily tempted to react to the problem before we respond to our hearts? We gloss over or, worse, we miss entirely how our hearts are becoming entangled by sin. Here are a few of the traps that ensnare us. Rather than being first responders to these crimes of the heart, we ignore them and begin correcting others.

Anger	Frustration	Fear	Dread
Angst	Complaining	Grumbling	Demanding
Disappointment	Regret	Self-Pity	Discouraged

Diagnostic Questions: Write out a prayer of praise to the Lord, thanking Him for revealing specific deceptions of your heart. Will you share what you wrote with a friend? How is this process beginning to change how you are thinking about your problem?

Step Six – Wrestle with the Lord

Your first call to action is to bring your heart to the Lord, asking the Spirit to dissect you so you can see the duplicity within, and then appeal to Him to appropriate the transformative work of the gospel that Jesus has provided for you.

These six steps must be how you begin working through conflict. Though you will not have all of your Spirit-illuminated sins eradicated, you will have them on the run. You are not looking for the perfection of God's sanctifying grace in your life, but you must have the presence of it.

God's grace must be actively working in your life, to the point where your response to trouble is filled with hope, not dread. Gratitude, not grumbling. Faith, not frustration. Only then will you become God-centered enough to be able to biblically problem solve. Let us review:

1. You see trouble as your opportunity to change.
2. This kind of humility positions you to address specific proclivities in your heart.
3. You begin a process of appropriating God's grace in your life.
4. You are now maturing through the trial rather than withering because of the problem.
5. Now, it is time to address the other person on the other end of the problem.

Diagnostic Question: How has this process changed the way you think about the other person? Hopefully, your attitude toward them has softened as the Lord addressed your imperfections. You now see yourself on somewhat equal footing before His cross.

Step Seven – Begin Thinking about Others

I am sure you have discerned by now how the hardest part of problem-solving and the bulk of the work needed to accomplish relational success is with you rather than the other person. The first six steps dealt with you and your heart. Does this strike you as odd, different, or wrongheaded? When trouble comes into your life, are you quicker to speak or quicker to listen (James 1:19)? Are you more willing to address the other person first, or do you choose to take your soul to task rigorously?

I wonder how different problem-solving would be if we were more rigorous with our hearts before we responded to others. I have observed that when I act like a knucklehead, by not addressing what the Lord is trying to teach me, I will make the original problem more complicated.

Call to Action

I gave you a list of negative traits for the problem-centered person earlier. Did you see yourself on that list? At the end of this chapter is a list of attributes for the God-centered person. An excellent way to assess yourself is by comparing your heart, attitude, words, and actions to that list.

Let's End Here: Are you problem-centered or God-centered?

This chapter focuses on how you should change when trouble comes to you. It is not about the other person(s) or even the problem. It is about how you relate to God and how He can work in your heart if you cooperate with Him.

Reminder: You are not looking for the perfection of these things but the presence of them. You will also notice how all of these attributes and characteristics have something to do with your faith in God. Read, pray, reflect.

Joy	Contentment	Rest	Confidence
Peace	Assurance	Gratitude	Wisdom
Discernment	Hope	Belief	Expectation
Progress	Contentment	Rest	Confidence
Encouraged	Responsive	Motivated	Obedient
Proactive	Stable	Encourager	Positive
Optimistic	Determined	Submitted	Endurance
Awareness	Illumination	Experience	God-Reliance
Moldable	Eschatological		

Chapter 9

Helping Your Friends

My friend, Eddie, performed his first funeral about three decades ago. He was a young preacher boy, who was nervous about the task before him. Funerals and weddings are some of the tensest and most self-aware public moments in our lives. As Eddie led the family and friends in prayer, he said,

"Father, it is so good for us to be here today."

That was a big oops. It was the wrong prayer for the occasion. Eddie had pulled out his trusty "so good to be at our church meeting" prayer, rather than his funeral prayer. Have you ever done that? When the time called for prayer #32, but you whipped out prayer #47?

There was nothing more for Eddie to do but to keep on praying—heads down and eyes shut, hoping he could stealthily switch prayer tracks in such a way that everyone would be blessed, rather than aghast. My friend's prayer story became humorous as time went by, but there are other moments when the things we say, especially during suffering, can create unhelpful memories that sting for a while.

Perhaps nothing is more misguided during the time of our suffering than when we are too quick on the draw with the "all things work together for good" line. It is not that Romans 8:28 is an inappropriate thing to say, but the timing of it can make all the difference. I remember when one of my friends pulled out his "8:28 bullet" during the darkest season of my suffering. Though I did not say this to him, what I wanted to come back with was,

"Has it ever occurred to you that I do not want all things to work out for good? I want my family back–my wife and my two children. I am aware how what I want and what the Lord is giving me right now are not the same things, but at this moment, I am not able to get on with the Lord's plans. I want my agenda right now (Isaiah 55:8–9)."

My theology was wrong, as well as my attitude, but I was also hurting. Sometimes it may be best to give your struggling friends a broader berth to imperfectly work out their salvation (Philippians 2:12). What other option do we have, but to develop our relationship with the Lord imperfectly when things fall apart? Though the goal is to be like Jesus, may we be honest? Being like Jesus is too high of a bar when we are wallowing in the depths of suffering.

We Three Friends

When it comes to how to do things wrong, probably the most criticized people in the Bible for giving inadequate counsel are Job's friends. It somewhat bothers me at the criticism they receive because I am not sure any of us (especially me) could do much better.

I feel for Job's friends about the same way I feel for Adam. I mean, who wants to be known as the guy who messed up the world? Imagine if it were the "fall of Rick" in the garden, and because of my slip up, we all are in this mess. We would no longer be Adamic but *Ricket*. Yikes!

I wonder what it will be like as we walk by Adam in heaven. What about Job's friends? Branding people for their mistakes is easy to do. What if we leveled the playing field? The truth is all of us have given poor advice. And if we continue to care for people, we are going to provide inadequate guidance in the future—especially when we have to come alongside our suffering friends.

- What would your counsel be to Job?
- How would you walk him through his ordeal?

I do not have an exhaustive list for you, but here are seven things I believe will serve you as you interact with your friends, who are going through situational challenges.

No "S" Word

Perhaps your friend sinned, and because of his sin, he is reaping personal suffering. It happens. And if that is the case, there is a time to bring up the sin in suffering, but it should not be the first thing that comes out of our mouths. Perhaps there was no sin committed, as in Job's case. If so, doing what Job's three friends did to him is wildly inappropriate. The most important "S" word to think about during suffering is suffering. Hug the sufferer. Let him know that you are there for him. Being there is where Job's friends got it right at the beginning. They did not say anything. They sat with their friend in silence.

"And they sat with him on the ground seven days and seven nights, and no one spoke a word to him, for they saw that his suffering was very great" (Job 2:13).

Be with Them

They were wise men. Just being there can make all the difference. There is something sacred and holy about "being" with another image bearer. "God with us" (Matthew 1:23; Genesis 39:2) is a significant aspect of the gospel, and when we image that to others, it is a beautiful thing. My friend, Randy, was Jesus for me. As the bad news was rolling in, I was being rolled over by the painful reality of what was happening to me.

Late one night, Randy knocked on my door. He said he was not sure why he came, other than the Lord placed me on his heart. He hardly said anything else to me. I was hysterical: Randy was quiet. Though it was nearly thirty years ago, I am still comforted by his presence that night.

Don't Trump Their Story

Too often in our effort to relate to others, we begin telling them our story. While there can be a place for connecting to another person with your life's narrative, it is more important to dive into their story, listening to their suffering—whatever it may be.

Sometimes you will hear this when someone says, "I know how you feel," and they launch into their experience. The truth is, the comforter does not know how you feel—not precisely. Personal suffering is unique to each person. The Lord relates to each of His children uniquely. It is not possible to accurately know how they feel because there are too many variables. The more important thing to do is find out how they feel. As appropriate and when the time is right, begin to draw the hurting person out. Try to understand how the Lord may be relating to them.

Listen to their suffering. There is a lot to learn. Guard your heart against mapping your experience over their experience. If you do not guard your tongue, you may begin to give them tips that worked for you, while missing the things the Lord wants them to hear and do.

Give Them Room

Nobody suffers perfectly. I did not mention earlier, but while Randy was in my home, I was walking around my house slamming my fist against the walls. When I found out my wife committed adultery, nobody could console me. My heart was bursting, as the most profound human trust in my life was shattered. Randy discerned this. He gave me space and time to be imperfect.

Giving imperfect people room to wobble can be wise. Expecting them to respond with Christlikeness is expecting too much and can place a burden on them to be what they can never be at that moment. I am not making a case for allowing a person to sin, but it may be possible for you to overlook what they are doing, especially if it is an episode rather than a pattern.

That horrible night was a unique one for me. It has been three decades since that night, and I have yet to walk through my house again beating my fist into the walls. Be discerning with your friends.

Remind Them of God

Hopefully, you will have the opportunity to begin realigning their theology. If you know them well and you are not planning on popping in and popping off, then please give them sound Bible wisdom like Romans 8:28.

The Lord is sovereign, and He is working good in their lives. More than likely your friend will know this, though he may not have this at the top of his mind at the moment. Rather than trying to come up with some new truth, it would be wiser to remind him of the old truth of the gospel. One of the most effective ways to connect with an individual is by speaking to their understanding and experience—to what they already know. The Lord does not need to be nuanced in a new and different way. Be plain, clear, and simple.

Give Them Hope

Talk to them plainly about the greatness of our God and the counter-intuitiveness of His ways. God's Word brings hope to the hurting soul. It is rare for a counselee to say, "Wow, I have never heard that before." More than likely they will say, "There is nothing you have told me that I did not already know." I would hope that would be the case.

It would be much harder if I told them things about God that they did not know. If so, I would have to build a theological foundation for them. Creating a doctrinal construct while trying to care for a person's soul is arduous and much more challenging than reminding a Christian of truths with which they already had a familiarity.

Pray with Them

Though prayer is assumed, you should not overlook or underrate it. It is not a tack on at the end of a meeting as though it was a routine Christian expectation. Prayer is the most powerful way you can engage Sovereign Lord, the one who is behind all of the sufferings we experience.

Prayer does many things. For example, it is an acknowledgment that the Lord is God and we are not. Knowing who God is becomes necessary because the sufferer may be broken but not humbled. There is a difference. The broken person can sit in the dust of his catastrophe while still relying on himself. The humble person can sit in the same place but humbly acknowledge his need for the Almighty.

With that kind of humility comes empowering favor from the Lord (James 4:6). The person who can pray with open hands and no hidden expectations is setting himself up for God to impose Himself into the suffering.

This kind of prayer-filled attitude softens the heart, which gives shape to the Father's will to grow inside of us rather than our agendas (Luke 22:42). The only way Jesus could index forward to His Father's will was through the portal of prayer.

Prayer also creates a trinitarian *koinonia* between the Lord, the sufferer, and you. When you three are in communion together, it is one of the most intimate things you can do, and the only way you and the sufferer can access God's strength for the moment.

Call to Action

What I have communicated here are a few ways that might help those you are serving. It is possible for the Spirit to move you differently. Discerning the Spirit is one of the keys you will need when you step into a unique suffering opportunity.

The other key is that you must do something. At the heart of the gospel is going, doing, moving, acting, loving, giving, serving, and helping. To do nothing when a person is hurting is "another gospel," not the one the Savior modeled for us. We must go to those who are hurting, seeking to enter into their pain.

My friend, Eddie, might not have had the perfect prayer opening, but he was willing to go, to care, and to give what he had for a hurting family.

Chapter 10

How Do You Want to Suffer?

All people born in Adam have no choice about personal suffering (Genesis 2:16–17). That is the bad news. The good news is we can choose whether we want to experience our problems with or without God.

It is so easy to forget how suffering comes with the "human package," a consequence of the fall of Adam (Philippians 1:29; 1 Peter 2:21). It is easier to forget how the Lord wants to walk with you through your suffering. Not knowing God while suffering certainly adds to the complexity of the troubled soul (Psalm 46:1). To be caught in the vortex of a spinning tornado and unsure if God is with you is suffering's most significant victory (Genesis 39:21).

"Behold, I go forward, but he is not there, and backward, but I do not perceive him; on the left hand when he is working, I do not behold him; he turns to the right hand, but I do not see him" (Job 23:8–9).

Job came to this point in his life. From his perspective, he was lost and without God. To top it off, he had no clue about the Father's back traffic conversation with the devil. He did not realize how no amount of praying was going to bring his problems to a successful conclusion.

105

- How does that make you feel?

- What are you thinking?

"The secret things belong to the Lord our God, but the things that are revealed belong to us and to our children forever, that we may do all the words of this law" (Deuteronomy 29:29).

Suppose the Lord was working a more profound and more mysterious plan in your life, and suffering was the vehicle He chose to carry out those greater purposes (Genesis 50:20).

When It's Your Time to Die

Job is only one of many people the Lord selected to suffer for His higher purposes (Hebrews 11:32). Your salvation happened because the Lord chose to allow suffering in the life of Jesus (Isaiah 53:10). Praise God there was no alteration or abating to the pain of Jesus until He finished the task (Genesis 3:15; Matthew 26:39; John 19:30).

I think most folks are okay with the benefits of the gospel (John 3:16) while praising God for the sacrifice of the gospel (2 Corinthians 5:21). The problem is when the practicalization of the gospel comes home to roost in our lives. That's when the call to suffer becomes your cross to bear (Luke 9:23).

It reminds me of Paul, a man who was in the midst of unrelenting suffering (2 Corinthians 12:1–10). In this sense, his suffering was somewhat parallel to Job's. The Lord used Satan to harass his servant (2 Corinthians 12:7). Paul promptly prayed three times for the pain to stop (2 Corinthians 12:8).

The Lord essentially said his trouble would not go away, so Paul discontinued his appeals for the cessation of his suffering. He learned how his thorn in the flesh was predetermined by God to buffet him and to teach him how to not rely on himself but rather to rely on Him who raises the dead (2 Corinthians 1:8–9).

Rather than relying on his prayers as a method to get God to change His mind, he began to rest upon the grace of God to propel him into a more profound experience and usefulness in God's kingdom. Paul said it this way:

"Therefore I will boast all the more gladly of my weaknesses, so that the power of Christ may rest upon me. For the sake of Christ, then, I am content with weaknesses, insults, hardships, persecutions, and calamities. For when I am weak, then I am strong" (2 Corinthians 12:9–10).

Rather than a complaining spirit, Paul had a boasting spirit. His understanding of the circumstances the Lord was permitting into his life transcended what was happening to him. It even changed what Paul wanted for his life. He saw a more significant prize through suffering rather than sublunary desires for planet living (Philippians 3:8).

I am not here to magnify Paul as though he was something special. Paul was an ordinary man as far as his humanness and temptations were concerned. What I hope to amplify is the grace of God that speaks to how He can turn pain into power.

We often read the Corinthian text and think that Paul was a great man and that he overcame his trials because of his specialness. This kind of thinking would be a travesty because it would marginalize

God's power while magnifying Paul's abilities (1 Corinthians 1:25; 2 Corinthians 4:7).

God's grace was sufficient for Paul, not the sheer will and courage of any perceived greatness that you may want to attribute to him. Paul could do all things through Christ who strengthened him, not through Paul who strengthened himself (Philippians 4:13).

From Praying to Complaining

In the middle of the Book of Job, you find another man who could not untangle himself from his misery. By this point in the book, he had a lot of good and evil counsel from his friends, as well as from his introspective turmoil. The singular constant through it all was unshakeable suffering.

As he continued to progress through his tribulation, the God that Job knew appeared to have left him. He vanished, so Job thought. Before his suffering, Job loved God and walked with Him. He served Him daily, and God was near, active, and reciprocal.

Shortly after the suffering came into Job's life, he began to separate himself from the God that he loved. I am not sure when Job perceived the distance that occurred between him and his Lord. Notice how he frames it at the mid-point of the book.

"Then Job answered and said: Today also my complaint is bitter; my hand is heavy on account of my groaning. Oh, that I knew where I might find him, that I might come even to his seat" (Job 23:1–2)!

* In Job 1:20–22 he prayed to God as an act of worship.
* In Job 23:1–2 he complained out of the emptiness of his soul.

His praying turned into complaining, and his complaining turned into bitterness, and his bitterness separated him from the Lord.

- Suffering + God = Hope and Empowering Grace
- Suffering – God = Complaining, Bitterness, Heaviness

Separation from God happens when you lose sight of where God is and what He is up to in your troubles. This kind of over-fixation on suffering leads to its magnification, which will eventually captivate your thoughts (2 Corinthians 10:3–6).

After this happens, the troubled soul becomes a complaining spirit. This tension is where you find Job. The heaviness of his soul lowered him into a dark hole from which he could not escape.

Bitterness: A Form of Self-Punishment

Job lost sight of God during his troubles, and his soul began to drift from what he believed (Romans 8:31–39). He went from a joy-filled position of God-centeredness to a frustrated perspective of problem-centeredness.

His suffering caused a prescribed misery in his life. It is one thing when God brings suffering to you, as he did with Job, but a whole other matter when a person's sinful response to God's work further compounds the misery.

Bitterness is not a medicine that helps you change or brings about a preferred life. Bitterness is a form of self-inflicted misery. It is a way of punishing oneself and others (Hebrews 12:15). It is poison for the soul.

Some writers accurately translate the word bitterness in this text as rebellion because bitterness is a form of rebellion against God. You cannot be bitter and be in harmony with God. Bitterness causes rebellion.

Whenever an individual persists with a complaining spirit, while refusing to repent of this sin, he willfully separates himself from God. I am not sure how perceptive Job was to what he was doing to himself or his relationship with the Lord, but his wrong attitude affected his soul. Job was right in that he could not find God in his trouble (Job 23:3). The reason for this was because of his bitter resistance to what God was doing in his life. He was willfully and unwittingly separating himself from God and then complaining because God was not near—a biblical conundrum.

1. I am hurt.
2. I complain.
3. My complaint turns to bitterness.
4. My bitterness is rebellion.
5. My rebellion separates me from the Lord.
6. I can no longer receive help from the only One who can help me.

Where to Find God

God was in Job's suffering. He was smack dab in the middle of it, persevering with Job on one hand while battling the devil on the other hand. Job would later learn this terrifying truth (Job 23:16). In time, it appears a glimmer of hope began to manifest into Job's mind. He was transitioning from the elusive possibility of a better day without suffering to the soul-wrenching option of experiencing God while in the crucible (Daniel 3:25).

"But he knows the way that I take; when he has tried me, I shall come out as gold" (Job 23:10).

If getting away from trouble becomes the focal point of your life, you may circumvent the beautiful things (Romans 8:28) the Lord wants you to experience, which you can only experience during your trouble.

It is within your "Adam-given scope and tendencies" to find the easy way out of trouble (Genesis 3:7–8). Running and hiding makes sense at the moment, but it may not be your best move.

If you are struggling to persevere through inescapable suffering, my challenge to you is to find the Lord. He is there. He is with you. He promised never to leave you (Deuteronomy 31:6; Matthew 28:20; Hebrews 13:5). Do you believe this?

Making your way back to God is a slow and laborious process. It requires you to set aside your preferred life for the life the Lord is giving you right now. If you do this, you will experience a new kind of grace.

It is overcoming grace, which comes proportionally and simultaneously to the degree you repent of any complaining and bitterness. This kind of experience with God will not happen until you enter into the ring with God (Genesis 32:24).

Are You Ready to Rumble (With the Lord)?

I would recommend you have many honest talks with Him. One of the refreshing things about this passage in Job is his honesty. His perspective needed adjusting, but his willingness to not hide his exact thoughts is encouraging.

Be honest with God. Do not hide from Him what He already knows about you (Hebrews 4:13). Denying the truth about yourself will mask the real you, and eventually you will lose contact with the ugly truth about who you are (Romans 1:18). Self-deception may feel right at the moment, but you will reap a harvest of bitter herbs if you persist in your blindness (Hebrews 3:7–8).

"They (Gentiles) are darkened in their understanding, alienated from the life of God because of the ignorance that is in them, due to their hardness of heart" (Ephesians 4:18).

Paul's appeal to the Ephesian Christians was to not be like the Gentiles, who were susceptible to "futile" thinking (Ephesians 4:17). This kind of mental manipulation is a path you do not want to travel. It is unfortunate enough to be bitter. It is worse when you can no longer perceive your sin (Hebrews 5:11). Job was explicit and articulate about his sin. He laid it out and began the process of wrestling through it with the Lord.

Initially, if you do this, you will not feel any change in your soul or your circumstance. Nevertheless, the Lord will enable you in ways that sheer human will cannot accomplish. Remember that you move forward by faith, not based on existential feelings.

I realize the things that I am saying are hard. Perhaps they are too hard for you. I understand. My appeal is for you to find a close and trusted friend, a small group leader, or a pastor who can walk with you through these challenges. The body of Christ is an invaluable resource when unwanted pain comes into your life. If the whirlwind of trouble has captured you, please reach out for help. There are more friends out there than Job's three buddies. Pursue Christ and His body.

Let these "means of grace" support you while teaching you how to appropriate His extraordinary power into your life. It is your choice: you can suffer with God or without God, but one thing is for sure: you will suffer.

Chapter 11

When God Is Not with You

The loneliness of being alone is a sting that penetrates to the depths of a person's soul. This kind of isolation is different from being by yourself. It cannot be solved by merely hanging out with people.

Being lonely is an isolating pain. It is more internal than external. Sometimes people talk about physical coldness that penetrates the body to where you are bone cold. This kind of physical chilling is similar to the spiritual feeling of loneliness that individuals experience on the inside. It reminds me of the curse of darkness Moses put on the Egyptians.

"Then the LORD said to Moses, 'Stretch out your hand toward heaven, that there may be darkness over the land of Egypt, a darkness to be felt'" (Exodus 10:21).

Even being in the middle of one hundred people does not bring relational warmth to the lonely soul because loneliness at its root is a spiritual matter. Though there is a physical component to a community, there is a more profound truth with the problem of being alone.

On the physical front, you associate and enjoy being around people. On the spiritual front, it is essential to connect with other spiritual beings at a level that pushes you beyond mere superficialities.

Sometimes you will hear people talk about their frustration with others who do not go deep into their relationships. Their complaint focuses on a desire to intersect with another person at the level of the heart. This hope is fantastic.

God created us for an external and internal community. Because He made us in His image, there is a longing within us to be like the Lord. God is the original community. Father, Son, and Spirit enjoy an uninterrupted, interpersonal relationship within the Trinity.

It made sense after the Lord created Adam to want to bless His creation by giving him a complementary helper (Genesis 2:18). We do not know all the detailed reasons the Lord did this for Adam, but we do know it was not best for him to be without human companionship, whether in marriage or within the human community.

God with Us

Our desire for community is a partial affirmation that God made us in His image: we are "similar" to Him. He is like us, and we are like Him (James 3:9). Humanity has a sense of and craving for tribal belonging.

The historical record seems to affirm this as we perceive the Lord's desire to hang with us. We see Him walking with Adam (Genesis 2:15–17, 3:8). Later, He asked Moses to build a tabernacle so that He could be with His people (Exodus 25:8).

When the family finally settled down in the land of Israel, the Lord gave instructions to Solomon to build something more permanent so that He could be with His people (1 Chronicles 22:10). The Son became a man so that He could be with us, to help us (Matthew 1:23; John 1:14; Hebrews 2:14–15). After He left us, He gave us the Spirit to live inside us so that we could continue our shared connection with Him (John 16:13–15; 1 Corinthians 2:14).

The best part of heaven is how we will be with and experience Him forever and ever. His gift to us is an unending reciprocal delight (Revelation 22:5). From beginning to end, the Lord has made way for His children not to be alone. Our external and internal being can be fully satisfied with God's plan for relationships.

1. We can experience physical and relational connectivity with God and others.
2. We can experience spiritual and relational connectivity with God and others.

God Not with Us

* Have you ever wondered what it would be like to live in a world without God?
* How would you feel if you did not know God, could not perceive God, or had no awareness of His presence?

Losing sight of God is a soul-altering experience. It is one thing when humanity disconnects from you, but the loneliness of being alone is when you do not sense the presence of the Lord in your life. You "feel" this kind of isolation.

The worst-case scenario of this is eternal separation from God in hell. But there can be an echo of hell on earth when you are relationally distant from Him. Job had this experience. Listen to his lonesome words.

"Behold, I go forward, but he is not there, and backward, but I do not perceive him; on the left hand when he is working, I do not behold him; he turns to the right hand, but I do not see him" (Job 23:8–9).

It was during my four-year journey with Job where I felt this kind of loneliness. After my wife and children left, I began to lose sight of the Lord. The complicatedness of this time tempted me to drift from Him. The soul-diminishing effect of being separated from the Lord took a mighty toll on me as I spiraled into a four-year "dark night" of mental and spiritual confusion. Like being snow blind, I could not perceive the Lord in any direction.

It was the worst time of my life from which I reluctantly resigned that I would never see a better day. I do not remember if I lost hope or if I gave up on hope. That awful season reminds me of a miserable song from the desperate and lost songwriter, Hank Williams, Sr. called "I'm So Lonesome I Could Cry." Enter into his darkness.

Hear that lonesome whippoorwill
He sounds too blue to fly
The midnight train is whining low
I'm so lonesome I could cry

I've never seen a night so long
When time goes crawling by
The moon just went behind the clouds
To hide its face and cry

Did you ever see a robin weep

When leaves began to die?

That means he's lost the will to live

I'm so lonesome I could cry

The silence of a falling star

Lights up a purple sky

And as I wonder where you are

I'm so lonesome I could cry

Job's misery took him to this level. He was so lonesome that he could cry, and he did. Job might have known God was near, but his complexing misery was exponentially more massive than his intellectual theology.

Find a Friend

Whenever your troubles are more controlling than the truths of Scripture, you are living in unbelief. This spot is where Job landed. I, too, became an "unbelieving believer." Though I had a theology degree on my wall, I perceived the Lord was no longer in my heart.

It was at that point that I read Job's desperate words (Job 23:8–9). As horrifying as his perspective was, it resonated in my soul. It was the first time in a long time that I no longer felt alone. Though I could no longer perceive the Lord with me, Job was becoming my new best friend, forever.

One of the beauties of Scripture is its unashamed willingness to reveal all the dark machinations of sin. It does not hold back from the good or the bad. Oddly, Job's troubles began to give me hope. He had been where I was (Ezekiel 3:15). It reminded me of another man.

"Since then we have a great high priest who has passed through the heavens, Jesus, the Son of God, let us hold fast our confession. For we do not have a high priest who is unable to sympathize with our weaknesses, but one who in every respect has been tempted as we are, yet without sin. Let us then with confidence draw near to the throne of grace, that we may receive mercy and find grace to help in time of need." (Hebrews 4:14–16).

Job began to reconnect me back to Christ. Sometimes God can appear to be so far from you that you need a friend to help you get back to your first love (Revelation 2:4).

My church friends abandoned me. Some of them did this because they shunned divorced people. Others were alienated from me because they felt awkward being around someone who should be married. And others did not know how to help me. In time, they all left, and I was alone.

This period was when the Lord invited me to His Word, specifically the Book of Job. The Spirit moved me to sift through His pages. Over time, this book became my cherished friend that slowly dissipated the darkness. It was my only friend. I spent days reading page after page.

In my loneliness, God revealed Job to me. This Old Testament sufferer walked off the pages of Scripture and into my life. I love this man. God used Job to help me get back to Him. I sat with Job many nights—four years total—and learned from him. I wanted to feel what he felt, see what he saw, and learn what he learned (Philippians 4:9).

I already knew the end of the story: God would eventually restore him (Job 42:10). Job was a success story. Knowing the hopeful end motivated me to persevere through the progression of pain, praying that my conclusion would be similar to my new friend (Philippians 1:6).

On Becoming Gold

Job was desperate and lost, but he eventually regained his wits. God was renewing his mind, even though he could not perceive the Lord in his troubles. Right after his declaration about not being able to find God (Job 23:8–9), he said,

"But he knows the way that I take; when he has tried me, I shall come out as gold" (Job 23:10).

We have to put this in perspective. Job was not yet golden. Job sat in lostness, loneliness, and anger. He did not become gold and then speak these great words as though his future hope had already come to pass. He spoke in faith while sitting in the loneliness of his lostness. Faith is an understanding of how things are going to be long before that desired and perceived outcome comes to pass.

"Now faith is the assurance of things hoped for, the conviction of things not seen" (Hebrews 11:1).

This perspective is key. Though the trials and challenges of your life can dull the truth you know, those problems should not overcome the reality of how God is actively working in your life. Your experience does not alter God's truth.

Just because you may not perceive Him, does not mean that He is not doing things on your behalf. You must own this kind of thinking if you are going to persevere through your troubles. You must daily bring God's Word to bear on your experience.

"Whatever is true, whatever is honorable, whatever is just, whatever is pure, whatever is lovely, whatever is commendable, if there is any excellence, if there is anything worthy of praise, think about these things" (Philippians 4:8).

This worldview is the essential first step in closing the gap in a distant relationship with the Lord. The battle begins in your mind, not in your circumstances. How is God's Word reshaping your thoughts?

Faith in God changes your misconceptions about God. This news is good because you need ongoing help to fully understand all the Father does to sanctify you as a Christ-follower. Not being able to perceive God in whole or in part should not be a hindrance to your relationship with Him. Do you believe God's Word (Deuteronomy 31:6; Hebrews 13:5)?

The Bible assures you how God is for you (Romans 8:31). You may not be able to recognize it today, but it does not alter the truth of God's Word. This Bible fact is what it means to live by faith rather than sight: when the truths of God's Word overcome whatever mood or feeling you are experiencing today, you are in the process of being transformed into gold.

"So we do not lose heart as we look not to the things that are seen but to the things that are unseen. For the things that are seen are transient, but the things that are unseen are eternal." (2 Corinthians 4:16–18).

"(Moses) endured as seeing him who is invisible" (Hebrews 11:27).

Seeing, knowing, and cherishing your great "invisible God" is at the heart of experiencing His presence when you're lonely.

Chapter 12

Ever Tried Manipulative Praying?

There is a unique place where good and evil intersect in a Christian's life. That place is personal suffering. What the world, flesh, and the devil mean for evil, the Lord God Almighty intends for your good (Romans 8:28).

A theocentric view of suffering makes personal pain the worst of times and the best of times, though we typically do not see the benefit in our suffering until it has long passed. Isn't this true for you? As you reflect upon the most painful times of your life, haven't you seen how the Lord was there sustaining and caring for you?

During suffering, you experience a grace that you cannot appropriate at any other time. When the Lord drives you into the crucible of suffering and magnifies Himself by sustaining you, it creates an indelible, soul-stirring memory. There is a deep intimacy found in the heart of God that you access through a cross that leads to your "death."

"That I may know him and the power of his resurrection, and may share his sufferings, becoming like him in his death" (Philippians 3:10).

I have talked to many Christians who have echoed this truth. Though they never want to go back into their crucible, they do acknowledge how they would not exchange their experience with God that came during their fiery trial (Daniel 3:20; 1 Peter 4:12).

I agree with them because it's my story, too. After my family had left, I went into a deep sorrow from which I did not fully return for ten years. The despair was unending. The confusion was spiritually disorienting. There are no words to describe the pain of those years.

I resigned my life to the lower shelf of the Christian ecosystem. As I looked into my future, I could see nothing hope-filled. It was dark, bleak, and unending. Hope was gone as I began to accept how the future would always look like my present.

It was in this place, where God's goodness entered into the suffering, that He gave me a new way of seeing things. Before this, I knew the Lord, but it was in the crucible of hopelessness where I experienced Him in a unique, unforgettable, and life-transforming way (Job 42:5–6).

Two Christian undergrad degrees did not introduce me to the Lord in the way I needed to know Him. Education gave me an awareness of theology, but unremitting anguish gave me Christ. Knowing the Lord intellectually and experiencing Him in life-altering pain are radically different things.

Batter My Heart

Intense suffering brings a convergence into your life that wants to tear apart your soul. It is fear and faith going toe-to-toe in a loser-leaves-town match. And you are never really sure who will win.

This kind of internal consternation is the most vulnerable and fertile ground for the Lord to affect you. It is in this sort of trial where He can put something in you that will never leave you, for which you will be eternally grateful and may reap the benefits for the rest of your life.

This perspective is why a person will look back on his most painful experience and say, "God was amazingly good to me at that time." If you have been there, I need not say more. I have just described your pain and your praise. You see the juxtaposition of this fear/faith, pain/praise tension in John Donne's Holy Sonnet, "Batter My Heart," where he pleaded with the Father to do whatever was necessary to transform him into a new creation:

> *Batter my heart, three person'd God; for, you*
> *As yet but knock, breathe, shine, and seek to mend;*
> *That I may rise, and stand, o'erthrow me, and bend*
> *Your force, to break, blow, burn and make me new.*

- Has God ever battered your heart?
- Do you want Him to do this for you?

Donne's sonnet is one of the most radical prayers a person can pray. Notice the progression of his thought. Initially, he asked the Lord to knock, breathe, shine, and seek to mend. Upon more reflection, he ratcheted up his desire for transformation when he asked the Lord to break, blow, burn, and make new.

- How desperate are you to experience the Lord, to be transformed by Him?

- How desirous do you think the Lord is to try you so that He can remove the things that hinder you from experiencing Him?
- Do you want your heart to be battered by God so that you experience transformation into someone who is radically different from who you are?

When Life Kills Your Dream

Les Miserables is one of my favorite Broadway shows. One of the characters in this play is Fantine, a lady who lived a most miserable life that ended too soon. Her song in the play is, "I Dreamed a Dream." Here is a stanza:

I had a dream my life would be
So different from this hell I'm living,
So different now from what it seemed.
Now life has killed the dream I dreamed.

For many of us, life kills our dreams. After we marry, we launch our covenantal boats toward a glistening horizon. Though we realize the potentiality of dark skies, we dismiss the notion because we would rather not think about it, or we believe we're different.

Even when we see the dark clouds forming in our lives, we do not perceive them for what they are, or we do not understand how the Lord may be about to teach us richer meanings of biblical faith.

I saw the dark clouds taking shape in our marriage but never realized the extent to which the winds were going to blow or how they would wreak havoc. I was in my second year of college, working on a Bible degree when God blindsided me while doing good. I cannot adequately explain to you the depth of the pain. Upon arriving home on April 8, 1988, I realized my family was gone. Within fifteen hours I had lost ten pounds. It was the most prolonged and most torturous night of my life. I was in the throes of unmitigated fear, desperation, and physical suffering.

My desire for a family fully collided with the Lord's willingness to reveal Himself to me in a way that necessitated death. It was my death He had in mind. I was confused and depressed about the story He was writing. During my time in Job, I read, meditated, prayed, and cried through his struggle. I will never forget the day when I arrived at chapter twenty-three and read these words:

"But he is unchangeable, and who can turn him back? What he desires, that he does. For he will complete what he appoints for me, and many such things are in his mind. Therefore I am terrified at his presence; when I consider, I am in dread of him" (Job 23:13–15).

My world stopped spinning long enough for me to hang on to every syllable out of Job's mouth. I was stunned when Job affirmed what I already perceived about God: He was changeless, and what He desires, He does. My thoughts went wild.

Let's Fake Out God

As I meditated on these terrible truths, my mind prematurely jumped to the end of the story—the happily ever after part. I learned how the Lord released Job from the crucible of suffering and how He blessed him with twice as much as he had before (Job 42:10).

Then I thought, "Maybe He will release me, too." Though I knew the Book of Job was not a prescription for how suffering happens, I desperately wanted his ending to be mine, too. This desire for a happy ending brought immediate hope because it offered a way out of the pain. All I needed to do was inform the Lord what needed to happen next.

It was time to update God. I needed to make Him aware of what I had learned and how I had changed. His mission to mature me was complete. My thinking was, "Maybe He does not know I have learned all these lessons. I must inform Him how he can remove the hounds from hell that were harassing me (2 Corinthians 12:7)."

"But he is unchangeable, and who can turn him back? What he desires, that he does" (Job 23:13).

I was okay with His unchangeableness and the fact that I could not budge Him. He just needed to know that His desire to change me had worked. "Lord, I am okay down here: everything is cool." Once He gets the update, He will pour out a better blessing, in a different way. I prayed:

Thank you, Father, for the privilege of suffering. You have taught me many amazing things, and I am grateful for the life lessons. You are merciful and kind to me. Your work in me has accomplished several good things, and I am now ready to move on to what you have planned for our next adventure. I await release from this suffering while looking forward to the fruitful ministry that it has caused.

Your grateful and humble servant,
Rick

There was a slight problem with my prayer. I knew in my heart that I was trying to manipulate God. The combination of desperation and hurt motivated me to prod God along, hoping He would expedite His plans for me.

I cannot say I was wittingly trying to fake out God—like anyone could accomplish that, but that was what I attempted to do in my ignorance. Sometimes the pain can be too much, even to the point of trying to circumvent the wisdom of God (1 Corinthians 1:18–25). Still, at some level of my heart, I knew this kind of praying would not work. The Lord was not through with me, and what He had planned for me would not be thwarted, regardless of how many times I prayed otherwise (2 Corinthians 12:8).

"He will complete what he appoints for me, and many such things are in his mind" (Job 23:14).

Game playing with the Lord will not work because He sees in the dark places of our hearts and He always gives us exactly what we need even if we do not want it. It did not matter if I agreed with Him: He was going to finish His desires for my life (Philippians 1:6).

My Father knew best, and no amount of manipulative praying was going to sway Him. The real issue for me was whether I would trust Him enough to cooperate with the necessary surgery on my soul, regardless of how long it would take (Hebrews 4:12–13).

Come Forth as Gold

Apart from salvation, this surgical season on my soul was the most transformative time in my life. Nothing has come close to the redemptive work the Lord did in me during those days. I reflect on how impossibly hard it was to get on board with His soul surgery. He saw things in me that I could not see (or did not want to see), and He loved me enough to persevere no matter how distracting or dishonest I was with Him.

The truth was that I knew how messed up I was on the inside, but I did not want to go through the necessary changes for transformation to happen. Perhaps you are like this, too. To some degree, we all have enough self-awareness to know we need the Lord's intervention.

Still, we are afraid of Him. The thought of having the Lord turned loose on our souls is terrifying. Knowing this is why you must be careful. If you are not wise here, you will be intellectually dishonest with yourself, with God, and with others.

My appeal is for you to be honest. Admit to the Lord what He already knows about you. Do not try to manipulate Him or others by acting ignorant about what He needs to do inside of you. Let Him have His way.

The truth is that you have no choice. The Lord will do what He wants to do to you, and He will complete what He has appointed for you (Philippians 1:6). As Job said, "There are many more things in His mind" (Job 23:14).

Call to Action

1. Are you struggling now? Are you in a relationship trial? Are you trying to ignore what God is telling you? Are you tempted to "manipulate" God and others, as though that were possible?

2. Suffering is impossibly hard, but do you see it as God's mercy to you? What are you learning about your Lord as you walk through this trial with Him?

Chapter 13

Benefits of a Silent God

Silence does not have to be a bad thing, even the silence of God. During the Lord's quietness, He can communicate some of the most profound truths if you're willing to listen.

Ultimately, you have to trust the Lord's wisdom in all matters of life because life does not function in a formulaic way. What was true one time is not true all of the time. The plans you laid made sense to you when you laid them, but the Lord redirects your paths, and sometimes His paths lead you (Psalm 23:3) to places you never anticipated.

"The heart of man plans his way, but the LORD establishes his steps" (Proverbs 16:9).

Human ingenuity and understanding cannot answer all of your questions because you serve an active God, who is always working in ways that you cannot fully understand or explain. This challenge is especially hard (and scary) when your plans fall apart and you face plant into personal suffering.

Typically, when this happens, you are tempted to make the point-of-focus on what you did wrong, or maybe you direct your disappointment toward the Lord because He did not meet your expectations. To falsify the character of the sufferer (you did wrong) and the character of the Lord (He did wrong) are not your best options.

Maybe you did not do anything wrong—or at least not crazy enough to warrant such suffering. Perhaps the Lord knows better than you do, so He redirects your path in such a way that brings pain into your life (2 Corinthians 12:7–10).

- Is it possible for the Lord to be up to something that can only come about through your suffering?
- Could the deep pain you are going through today be the tapestry the Lord will use to show the beauty of His plans for you?

These are useful truths to consider as you reflect on His mysterious and good intentions for you. The real issue for you to ponder during these times of suffering is the silence of God.

- Why does the Lord not tell you the plans He has for you?
- Why does He have to be silent?

The Silence of God

Silence does not mean a lack of leadership. Just because God is not speaking to you, it would be wrong to assume He is not leading you. Leadership is verbal, and leadership is silence. It can be either because there are times when it is essential for the Lord to choose silence over speaking.

We see this in Job 28, where our old friend was in need of wisdom so that he could figure out what was going on in his life. He just went through twenty-five chapters of back-and-forth with his friends, which led him to nowhere. The Lord was mysteriously silent through all of this jabbering, and Job was well-aware of God's quietness. He was hungry for the words of God and weary of the wisdom of men (Job 12:2).

"But where shall wisdom be found? And where is the place of understanding?" (Job 28:12).

"From where, then, does wisdom come? And where is the place of understanding? It is hidden from the eyes of all living and concealed from the birds of the air" (Job 28:20–21).

Job knew that he needed wisdom and that it would come from the Lord, but he could not find God or His wisdom in his mess (Job 23:3). You are hurting and struggling, and the Lord is keeping His cards close to the vest. So, Job cries, "Where is wisdom?"

The Wisdom of God

Wisdom is living in a skill that is active, moving, and doing. Wisdom is not passive or static. It does not sit still. Wisdom gives you what you need so that you can actively respond to God and others. It is an ever-increasing and maturing knowledge you actively apply in the milieu.

Wisdom is not a philosophical idea or preachy cliché, but a theologically precise, active practice of God's work through you and into your life context. Wisdom is the thing you need a lot of to do life well. And Job did not have it.

His life fell apart, and he needed the active wisdom of the Lord to put his life back together again. And this is where it gets interesting on our journey with Job. The Lord does answer his query for wisdom. For the first time since the beginning of the book, the Lord speaks,

"Behold, the fear of the Lord, that is wisdom, and to turn away from evil is understanding." (Job 28:28).

Hey, are you looking for wisdom? You will find wisdom located in the fear of the Lord. Did you expect that? Did you know that? There is an inseparable connection between the wisdom of the Lord and the fear of the Lord.

You gain wisdom by actively walking on the "path of life" with the Lord, and the fear of the Lord is how you walk on that path. The two are inseparable. Without the fear of the Lord, you will not be wise.

The Fear of God

The fear of the Lord means to take Him seriously, knowing He alone is wise and powerful. It is a contrite recognition that you are not wise or strong (1 Corinthians 1:25). Because of who He is, you can trust Him fully in all ways and to any degree.

God is God, and you are not. The fear of the Lord is not to be afraid of Him but to be afraid of yourself. It is a simultaneous recognition of who you are and who He is while discerning the ginormous difference between these polar opposites. This kind of serious respect for the Lord brings humility to the soul.

The fear of the Lord and the wisdom of the Lord work together as cause and effect. The fear of the Lord (cause) produces the wisdom of the Lord (effect).

Without a right fear of the Lord, a person will not be able to gain wisdom from the Lord. The result for such a person will be ongoing and unremitting frustration in his life and relationships.

Job was not taking God as seriously as he should have been. He was popping off at the mouth, lacing his words with accusations. His lack of a proper fear of the Lord kept the wisdom of the Lord veiled.

The Help of God

The Lord can see things that you do not understand. Like any parent, there is wisdom and understanding that a child cannot possess. It is the child's responsibility to trust beyond their knowledge and awareness of how things ought to be. If the child does not have a sober assessment of what they lack and what their parents possess, he will miss the wisdom of the parents, and his life will be more complicated than it needs to be.

There are many things a parent would like to tell his or her child, but only when the child is genuinely broken and is humbly asking can the parent speak with authority and clarity. If the child does not have proper reverence for the parent, the parent may choose silence because it is obvious the child is not willing to listen. The child's lack of reverence for the parent shuts him out from the wisdom of the parent.

Some would argue, "I have been seeking the Lord. I have been asking for His wisdom. I want to know His thoughts and plans for me." No doubt all of these things are true, but this is where it will become hard for you.

If the Lord is silent, it is because He is rooting something out of you. There have been many times in my life where I uploaded "seeking the Lord" with self-preserving motives and agendas (Luke 22:42).

I was not mature enough or genuinely desirous enough to hear what I needed to hear, and the Lord was silent. There was no use for Him to speak because I laced my motives with self. The Lord's silence in my situation was not because He was mean. He was wise and loving. He knew how the thoughts and intentions of my heart were not pure (Hebrews 4:12–13).

The silence of the Lord lasted as long as I persisted in holding on to what I wanted more than what He knew was best for me. In my heart of hearts, I knew I was not willing to relinquish my plans entirely. The search for wisdom and its application happens through the process of elimination. The more you eliminate what you want, while thrusting yourself on the Lord—regardless of the cost, the more wisdom you will enjoy.

When suffering happens, a typical first response is to manage and control the situation in such a way that makes sense to the individual. Rather than seeking wisdom from the Lord, the person leans into his understanding.

"Trust in the LORD with all your heart, and do not lean on your own understanding. In all your ways acknowledge him, and he will make straight your paths. Be not wise in your own eyes; fear the LORD, and turn away from evil" (Proverbs 3:5–7).

It is not so much that the Lord is silent as it is that the person is not listening to what he needs to hear. It is the silence of God that leads to the required answers. As your ways prove futile, you begin a process of coming to an end of yourself. This "end of yourself" is the beginning of wisdom.

Once you are out of options and your plans are completely ruined, you turn to the Lord. Then you are ready to listen. Much like the prodigal son, you have to do it your way, and only when your ideas lead you to more desperation, you determine to be silent and listen to God (Luke 15:17).

Call to Action

1. Are there still traces of "my will" in your plans?
2. Are you willing to have all your motives and agendas laid before the Lord?

I am not making an accusation here as much as a confession. It is hard to talk unashamedly about the possibility of how we may be self-deceived, especially during the hard spots in life.

Sometimes we can want something so badly that we cannot see how our self-deception is bending our thinking in wrong directions. We are hurt, lonely, and afraid. And God is silent. In nearly every case, His silence is because we will not let go of something that we want—something He knows is not best for us. Even when we discuss those things among friends, we can become feisty, nasty, and accusatory.

It takes a lot of "humble desperation" to lay all of your cards on the table. If you are not willing to be that honest, you will cut yourself off from the wisdom of the Lord. This life intersection is where two of the more important questions you should be asking your friends are,

1. What do you perceive about me that I may not be recognizing about myself?
2. Will you help me see what I cannot see?

This step is the beginning of wisdom when you are willing to hold all of your ideas loosely while asking the Lord to use others to shake you from the things that have captured your heart.

The depth of self-deception and self-loyalty is more complicated and binding than any of us want to believe. Imagine if your child (if you are a parent) came to you and asked those two questions. You would most definitely cease from silence because two things would be true:

1. They respect you, as evidenced by taking you seriously, knowing you are wise and helpful. They have a contrite recognition that you are for them (Romans 8:31).

2. They want your wisdom, not their own. They are willing to let go of any hint of selfishness, regardless of the cost. They trust you.

Sometimes the silence of the Lord is the best thing for you. The key will be how you steward His silence. If you are experiencing the silence of the Lord, one of the best things you can do is find a place where you can have your motives and agendas carefully examined.

Through the Lord's silence, you are seeing an aspect of Job that was not clear when you first met him. As you progress through the rest of his book, all of Job's hidden motives will be brought to the light. After they are, Job will experience transformation when God finally speaks.

Chapter 14

Want to Know What God Thinks?

There are times when God can seem distant and seemingly disinterested about what is happening in our lives. On the ground level, we feel all alone. We are muttering and sputtering through life, while God is off fighting battles that seem more important to Him than tending to our business.

"And at noon Elijah mocked them, saying, 'Cry aloud, for he is a god. Either he is musing, or he is relieving himself, or he is on a journey, or perhaps he is asleep and must be awakened'" (1 Kings 18:27).

- Does God care about you?
- Is He paying attention?

You may be tempted to make futile attempts to force His hand through manipulative praying like I was. The truth is that you cannot budge God if He does not want to move, and what He has planned for you will most certainly be brought to pass (2 Corinthians 12:7–9; Philippians 1:6).

"But he is unchangeable, and who can turn him back? What he desires, that he does. For he will complete what he appoints for me, and many such things are in his mind" (Job 23:13–14).

Other times you may want God to intervene so badly that you do not give careful consideration to what it could be like if He did speak to you. The problem with this scenario is if your thoughts are not His thoughts, you may be in for the shock of your life when He finally gives His assessment about your situation (Isaiah 55:8–9).

Without question, circumstances demand an answer. And the Lord is the only one who knows all the answers. The problem is when you think you know the right answer and demand from Him to weigh-in on your troubles.

Sometimes I think it would be wise to be more cautious and discerning when requesting the Lord to reveal all of His cards to you. I am not suggesting you resign yourself to a twisted, morbid fear of God or to lace your thoughts with an accusation that suggests He is not for you (Romans 8:31).

God is for you. He is on your side. The Lord's favor on you and pleasure with you is never in doubt. God loves you with an everlasting love, and you cannot, in any way, diminish His affection for you. What I am suggesting is that you should perceive a wise and careful consideration about how you think about your problems. More than likely, whatever you are going through has more contours than you ever imagined.

The Lord is meticulously attentive to your life. He is more attentive to your life than you are. His omniscience allows Him to know every microscopic detail of your inner being (Hebrews 4:12–13) while simultaneously planning every future step and outcome (Proverbs 16:9).

Tread carefully about how you think about your problems. The Lord knows more than you, and He is doing more than you could ever think or imagine (Ephesians 3:20). If you are not careful, especially during seasons of suffering, you could develop a self-righteous, grumbling spirit that will cripple what the Lord desires to do in your life.

The Rest of the Story

"Then the LORD answered Job out of the whirlwind and said: 'Who is this that darkens counsel by words without knowledge? Dress for action like a man; I will question you, and you make it known to me. Where were you when I laid the foundation of the earth? Tell me, if you have understanding'" (Job 38:1–4).

The Lord was teaching Job the blessing of not knowing the rest of the story.

- Has it occurred to you how it is not a bad thing to not know the rest of the story?
- How easy is it for you to cast your cares on the Lord, even when life is not going according to your desires?

Job was aware that there were many things in the Lord's mind for him, and he knew God would bring those ideas to pass (Job 23:13–14). He even admitted how this kind of God-awareness terrified him to the point of making his heart weak (Job 23:15–16).

Still, yet, our old friend kept pressing for answers and his friends kept offering their counsel. Through it all, God was mysteriously silent. Like a father listening to his children argue from another room, the Lord sat in all His unbudgeable-ness as the faulty wisdom of His children was being bandied from one to the other (Job 12:2).

Then, in the perfect though seemingly slow timing of the Lord, He contributed a piece of His mind to Job's situation (Job 38:1–4).

Oh, my.

I must admit this is not what I was expecting from the Lord. Job was awakened from his wisdom-less "slumber" as counsel from heaven thundered down on his soul. And it only became worse from there. The Lord stood on Job's "proverbial neck" and did not relent for four contiguous chapters.

God went from silence to communication at the speed of sound, and the words He selected for His "above reproach" servant were some of the most reliable counsel you will ever hear. Apart from a brief response from Job (Job 40:3–5), the Lord gave one of His most extended counseling monologues in Scripture.

Divine Request to Be Quiet

This monologue is an amazing and mind-bending response from the Counselor to the counselee. It was one very long, rhetorical, mouth-stopping question after another. It was a divine request for Job to close his mouth and listen because he was talking way too much. Job's words had gone from a desire to figure out what was happening to him to a complaining and grumbling spirit (Deuteronomy 29:29).

If you put off fully trusting the Lord, especially when life does not make sense, you will eventually experience transformation into a bitter person (Matthew 6:34). Regardless of your good intentions, the Lord is not required to give you the answers to your most perplexing questions.

His call is for you to trust Him, which is so hard for our modern culture to understand and accept. The expectation of rights and privileges are so numerous that even an inconvenience at a traffic light can send an individual into a whirlwind of frustration.

It amazes me at this point in my walk with the Lord how I still complain about things that should not matter. After a while, it seems as though I would be mature enough to trust the Lord in all things, especially after experiencing Him work in some of the more difficult challenges of my life.

I was not always kind, patient, or understanding when I presented my arguments to Him, even though He was kind, patient, and understanding. He tolerated me. Sometimes I thought He was too patient—a nice way of saying that I thought He was too slow in coming to my side.

Regardless of my immaturity, He was unmovable, never giving in to seeing things my way. He would allow me to complain while He maintained His position of silence. This posture only irritated me while pushing me farther down the funnel of depression and discouragement.

Not to be deterred, the more silent He became, the more emboldened I became about my rights, my losses, and my need to know why these things were happening. If He was not going to speak, I maintained a torrid pace of filling up our time together with words.

Then the Lord Spoke

I will never forget the day, during my journey through Job, when I came to chapter thirty-eight, and the Lord finally said something. It was as though God was no longer talking to Job, but He was speaking to me.

Those unrelenting and demanding questions He was asking Job were questions for me. He began to remind me of a few things I had forgotten. My arrogance, coupled with a lack of faith toward His active goodness in my life, kept me from seeing all I needed to see.

This time I was silent. After the Lord broke the silence and entered into my whirlwind, it became fearfully apparent how I needed to shut-up, sit-up, and listen. If there was anything to say, it needed to be something like what Job said:

"Behold, I am of small account; what shall I answer you? I lay my hand on my mouth. I have spoken once, and I will not answer; twice, but I will proceed no further" (Job 40:4–5).

Sometimes your complaining may motivate God to respond to you. Beware: this could be a bittersweet experience. If you continue to demand from the Lord to reveal His full mind on your situation, let me ask you this question: "Do you really want to know what the Lord is thinking?"

What Job did not understand was how God could not and would not tell him all he wanted to know. Job could not know there was a deal struck with the devil and how the Lord was testing his faith (Job 1:12). The point of it all was supposed to be a mystery to Job because the Lord was teaching him to live by faith rather than by sight (2

Corinthians 4:18; Hebrews 11:27). The Lord cannot and will not tell you the outcome of the events in your life.

If you knew the outcome, you might endure. The problem with your endurance is that your faith would be in the known result rather than in the Lord Jehovah God. This situation would be contradictory to the first commandment (Exodus 20:3): your faith would not be in God alone.

God is calling you to a place of faith, which is the whole point of the Bible and your life. Trusting God was the point of the story with Adam and Eve—all the Lord asked from them was to believe Him (Genesis 2:16–17).

Put in His Place

Job wanted explanations for his troubles rather than trusting God who was in his problems. The Lord was not going to allow this. Knowing the answers would have put Job on the fast track to self-reliance, rather than trusting God (2 Corinthians 1:8–9). But Job would not shut his mouth.

His ongoing bitterness and complaining motivated God to bring clarity to the situation. Job received what he wanted, but it was not what he was expecting. The Lord put him in his place.

The Lord said, in a loud and relentless way, that there was only one option: trust Me! God was entirely in charge of the situation, and Job needed to trust Him. There is no counter-argument. You either believe the Lord through your circumstances, or you suffer the consequences. If you try to manhandle your problems your way, the Lord will be against you (James 4:6).

The good news for Job is that he listened. Job received the message loud and clear. He became quiet. He put his hand over his mouth. He stopped complaining. After the Lord spoke, there was nothing more to say.

What You Can Learn

Hopefully, you can learn from our old friend. There is wisdom from Job's story that you should be able to apply to your life practically. For example, though the Lord spoke, it did not change Job's circumstance one iota. God did not speak because He wanted to improve Job's situation. He spoke to change Job.

You will eventually see how God changed Job's heart (Job 42:5–6). You will also see how the Lord transformed his circumstances (Job 42:10), but a situational improvement was not the point of God's counsel at this moment. I cannot think of a time in my life when I thoroughly knew why I was going through a particular trial. Reflecting back, I can see how understanding the why was not the most critical thing the Lord wanted to reveal to me.

The most important thing to learn was how He was with me and would never let me go no matter how hard things became. If you can learn this one lesson, you will become a mature Christian, even if your circumstances never change. Do you really want to know what the Lord is thinking? If so, I suggest you put on your seatbelt because God's words might not go like you hoped, especially if you have been critical, grumbling, or faithless.

Chapter 15

When God Whittles You Down to Size

My former neighbor, Mr. Campbell, loves to carve. He has a fantastic talent for taking the nothingness of a stick and turning it into something special. Shortly after the first Christmas of our daughter, Tristen, I was dragging the Christmas tree to our backyard to get rid of it. Mr. Campbell saw what I was doing and asked if he could have the tree. It had no more value to me, so I gave it to him. After a while, I had forgotten he took our tree.

One Year Later

The following Christmas, Mr. Campbell knocked on our door. To my surprise, he was standing there with a beautiful hand-carved walking stick, which was about the size and shape of a baseball bat. At the top of the stick was a beautifully detailed carving of a Santa's head. On the side of the stick were these words:

"Tristen's Very First Christmas Tree, 2001."

Mr. Campbell took our used and useless tree and carved a beautiful walking stick to commemorate our daughter's first Christmas. We were humbled and surprised by what he did. Mr. Campbell said,

"I went down to the creek and sat on my bench. Then I began to ask, 'What is inside this tree?' So, I sat and started carving, and this is what I found inside your tree."

- He sat.
- He whittled.
- He took off some good wood and some knotted wood.
- He kept carving until he came to what he was hoping to find.

The discovery inside our useless tree was a treasure nobody else could see (2 Corinthians 4:7). I did not see it. My wife did not see it. Tristen did not see it. Only the master craftsman had a vision of what it could be.

After months of curing the tree in the heat of the summer and a few days of carving through the fall, Mr. Campbell unveiled the previously hidden treasure. The process was long and hard, but the woodcarver knew what he wanted, and he had the skill and patience to bring it to pass.

Whittled Down to Size

There are no appropriate analogies for what Job experienced in the final chapter that documents his journey. My tree story is a small attempt to convey a big idea. This closing segment of Job's journey gives us a transparent, humble, and vulnerable picture of a broken man. His life had been stripped down to where there was seemingly nothing left that separated him from his Maker.

The losses were many. The complaints were bitter and unending. The advice was insufficient. Job had finally come to the end of himself. He was not attempting to manipulate God any longer. He was not living in a self-caused, self-deception. He said it this way:

"I had heard of you by the hearing of the ear, but now my eye sees you; therefore I despise myself and repent in dust and ashes" (Job 42:5–6).

- His family was gone.
- His land was gone.
- His cattle were gone.
- His complaining was gone.
- His self-righteousness was gone.

He had no more questions: those left him, too. Job stopped talking, and God transformed his heart. Job met God.

He was stripped down, naked, and prostrate in the dust from where he came (Genesis 2:7; Ecclesiastes 3:20). Job was finally ready to not only hear the Lord but to see Him in a way that few people experience. The Father carried Job through a terrifying and complicated time. He brought him to a place in their relationship that words could not describe (Romans 8:26). Sometimes verbal-ness can complicate things. It was time for Job to be quiet and experience the terrifying greatness of God.

God and I Time

It was Job and God.

Alone.

The Lord had His man where He wanted him, and Job was content to be there—empty-handed, broken-hearted, and ready to learn.

"For you will not delight in sacrifice, or I would give it; you will not be pleased with a burnt offering. The sacrifices of God are a broken spirit; a broken and contrite heart, O God, you will not despise." (Psalm 51:16–17).

Everything Job used to be was now gone. The old Job was dead. He was dead to himself. His dreams, needs, desires, hopes, and expectations were all demolished, flattened, and removed by God. Job, like Paul, could say,

"I have learned in whatever situation I am to be content. I know how to be brought low, and I know how to abound. In any and every circumstance, I have learned the secret of facing plenty and hunger, abundance and need. I can do all things through him who strengthens me" (Philippians 4:11–13).

He began his journey with many personal blessings. In time, God ripped all of those good things away from him. Job sinned in response to what was happening to him. He was understandably dazed and confused. Even with the more profound needs of his soul not being met, his dismay and crying did not alter God's plans for him. Through it all, the Lord persevered with Job.

Job could not perceive the things that were wrong with him. Only the Lord had the depth of vision to see what was wrong with his servant and what only He could change. And He would not release His servant until He completed the task.

Exposed by God

Job and I are similar in that we both can be self-deceived. We cannot see what we need to see. We need someone looking into our lives, who loves us enough to do whatever it takes to change us. The Lord is such a person.

My problem is not only my self-deception. If I were honest, I would admit I do not want to be entirely known for who I am. Even under the light of God's omniscience, I tend to hide (Genesis 3:10; Hebrews 4:13).

Ironically, I cannot fool Him who sees in the dark. And He does not recoil with this knowledge of me or use it against me (Romans 8:1). The Lord is intentional and meticulous when it comes to the soul-shaping exercise of discipleship. This truth is why He is compelled to strip me down from time to time. He wants me to see what He sees. He wants me to know what He knows. He does not do this because He is mean or because He has a desire to toy with me. He does this because He loves me.

- Have you ever been stripped down by God?
- Have you ever had the life-transforming experience of being hoisted upon the wood carver's bench for a season of pruning and reshaping?

There are times in our lives when we need the hindrances in our lives removed for His glory and our good. The impediments I am referring to are not necessarily the external things we accumulate.

The removal of external things, as in Job's case, was only the precursor to the more in-depth work the Lord wanted to accomplish in his soul. Imagine if the only thing the Lord did was to allow the devil to destroy Job's family and possessions. Those losses would affect him, of course. But there was a more profound work needed—an action designed to bring His servant into a more useful representation of Christ.

Beyond the Tipping Point

When the master Woodcarver begins to carve on us, He reveals the real person. Our disorientation, confusion, and anger are used to show the hidden and sinful elements of our lives. These wrong responses to the Lord's work highlight secret sinful conditions that need His redemptive solutions.

The Lord has to push us past the tipping point to reveal to us who we are. Being pushed past our self-sufficient limits is the only real way for the Lord to expose us. There is a famous quote within the Christian community that goes like this:

"Sin will take you farther than you want to go, keep you longer than you want to stay, and cost you more than you want to pay." — Unknown

What if you flipped the coin over and applied it to the Lord, as it pertains to the sovereign suffering He allows in our lives? Maybe it would sound like this:

"The Lord will take you farther than you want to go, keep you longer than you want to stay, and the process will cost you more than you could ever pay." —Rick Thomas

From God's perspective, He has no choice but to push us past the tipping point. We are too stuck on ourselves for it to be any other way. This concept was the message of Paul as he explained to the Corinthians why his team felt pushed to the point of death.

"For we do not want you to be ignorant, brothers, of the affliction we experienced in Asia. For we were so utterly burdened beyond our strength that we despaired of life itself. Indeed, we felt that we had received the sentence of death. But that was to make us rely not on ourselves but on God who raises the dead" (2 Corinthians 1:8–9).

Paul did not want the Corinthians to be ignorant of the despair they were experiencing. He had learned the lesson of Job: the Lord loves me so much that He will go to great lengths to save me from myself.

The Gold Standard

Job intellectually knew about the Lord—he had heard of Him by the hearing of the ear. He knew so much about the Lord that he could assume he would be okay (Job 23:10). He was confident the Lord would bring him through the fire (1 Peter 4:12). What he could not perceive was the difference between knowing the Lord and a fuller, unhindered experience with the Lord—"now my eye sees You."

Part of this process was the Lord taking Job from the subtle self-deceived thinking that he was something to a person who realized he was nothing, deserved nothing, and could be satisfied with nothing but God.

For Job, the mission was almost accomplished. He had gone from a man who believed he deserved better to a man who loathed himself.

He was beginning to find spiritual wholeness in human emptiness. Are you finding spiritual wholeness in human emptiness?

Job was stripped down naked. The Lord removed everything in his life that made him something. He fell apart as God exposed his soul for what it was. The Lord permitted him to agonize in such a way that revealed his well-hidden sin.

Through the agony of soul, Job was becoming a pliable man in the hands of his careful and loving heavenly Father. In time, he grew to the point of accepting and embracing the blessing of nothingness. Are you accepting and embracing the blessing of nothingness?

Rather than complaining about his suffering, he could see beyond his pain. God had broken him enough so that he could rely on the Lord in a way he had never experienced before. You could say that he transcended his suffering. He was in the "God zone."

It is hard for us to see beyond our suffering. We choose to be suffering-centered, as evidenced by talking more about our defeats than the Lord's victories. Are you living in the Lord's victories that are beyond your suffering? We tend to either get stuck at the future possibility of suffering or we get stuck in the current realities of suffering. Fortunately, the Book of Job not only gives us a peek into the pain but a pathway through the pain.

What we learned about Job in the first chapter was correct: he loved God. What we see in this last chapter is that he still loves God. Job loved God when he had plenty, and he learned to love the Lord when he had nothing. More importantly, God loved Job, and He would not let go of His servant. The lesson for us is to know that whatever the

Lord takes us through, He will love us to the end. He will never give up on us.

This kind of love is more comprehensive than most of us realize. It is this kind of love that will motivate Him to whittle us down to size until He has removed all the things that hinder us from experiencing Him in full measure. You may ask, "When will this process end?"

Only the Woodcarver knows how to form Christ in you, but be assured: He will complete this process one way or the other (Philippians 1:6). An excellent way for you to self-assess your cooperation with Him through the process of personal suffering is to answer these two questions:

1. Do I respond in faith to my problems—am I trusting and resting in the Lord?

2. Or, do I respond in fear—am I anxious and complaining about what He is writing into my life?

How you answer these questions will give you a clue as to how much more whittling the Woodcarver has to do.

Chapter 16

Looking beyond Your Suffering

Does anyone love God because of who He is exclusively, or do we love God for what we can receive from Him? More personally, do you have faith that is larger than your self-interests?

This question was the accusation of the devil to the Lord about Job. There is something genuine about this kind of charge because it resonates in everyone's heart. Christians love the Lord, but they are not so self-deceived to discount self-loyalty. Why do you serve the Lord?

I know part of the answer is because divine sovereignty imposed Himself on your life and made you born again if you are a Christian (John 3:7; Ephesians 1:4). Ultimately, that is the number one answer—God regenerated you. But personal salvation does not fully dislocate your depravity. There are always other motives lurking in imperfect hearts. Nobody is free from sin's temptations.

"Wretched man that I am! Who will deliver me from this body of death?" (Romans 7:24).

The irony here is that we want to be free from the complexity in our souls, but we do not want to go through the process to be free because the most effective way to be free is to suffer.

"In this you rejoice, though now for a little while, if necessary, you have been grieved by various trials, so that the tested genuineness of your faith—more precious than gold that perishes though it is tested by fire—may be found to result in praise and glory and honor at the revelation of Jesus Christ" (1 Peter 1:6–7).

Nothing will draw out your true motivations like personal suffering. The refining fire refines the soul. When God throws you into the crucible of suffering, every good and bad thing in you will eventually be made known. What has your suffering drawn out of your heart? For example, pain can reveal anger, fear, and the quality of your faith.

We want to be set free from sin, but we fear the process of being set free. This dilemma is our angst, which is why we need sovereign clarity, so we do not miss the lessons we are supposed to learn through the hard times that come to our lives.

Job went to the Lord's counseling office. And like any good counselor, the Lord drew out of Job's heart what Job needed to see. Collected together, the Lord asked Job seventy questions, all of which you could sum up this way:

"If God is big enough to keep you from suffering, isn't it also true, that He's big enough to have reasons for suffering that you do not understand?"

Unkindly, He Kindly Shows

There is wisdom to be found in that statement, but it is the kind of wisdom that does not come exclusively from an intellectual understanding of the Lord. The type of wisdom that I'm talking about comes from a deep and soul-exhausting experience with the Lord. Job said it this way,

"I had heard of you by the hearing of the ear, but now my eye sees you" (Job 42:5).

God taught Job about Himself. Job knew God. He received the Lord's instruction. He learned how the Lord gives and the Lord takes away things (Job 1:21). He knew faith comes by hearing and hearing by the Word of God (Romans 10:17). Job, like us, was Christianized enough to have a basic understanding of the Lord. What Job did not know was the difference between knowing God and seeing God.

It was only after his undeserved and horrific ordeal that he experienced the Lord in a unique way that transcended his previously known knowledge. When it comes to your relationship with God, you cannot see without hearing, but you can hear without seeing (Hebrews 11:27).

This twist is the difference between being in religion and being in a relationship with God. It is the difference between knowing the Lord through an intellectual intake and having an intimate fellowship that is born in the crucible of suffering.

"That I may know him and the power of his resurrection and may share his sufferings, becoming like him in his death" (Philippians 3:10).

Many people sit in church facilities every Sunday of their lives and hear many great things about the Lord, but their relationships with the Lord are no more profound than what they have heard. You must season your knowledge of the Lord in the fires of suffering for you to mature. The Lord took Job deeper than mere knowledge. It was a place that transcended language. A place where God shattered the idols of his heart.

"My idea of God is not a divine idea. It has to be shattered time after time. He shatters it himself. He is the great iconoclast (a person who attacks). Could we not almost say that this shattering is one of the marks of his presence?" —C. S. Lewis

- In every one of us, there are wrong ways of thinking about God, life, and others that can only be rooted out through suffering.
- In every one of us, there are selfish ways of thinking that we'll only see when God does not act like we think He should.
- In every one of us, there are selfish ways of thinking that motivate us to serve God for our good rather than His glory.

"So you think God was kind to make you sick?" Jemimah asked, "and take away your health and all your sons and friends, and daughters— all the ones you loved?"

"Jemimah, what I think is this: The Lord has made me drink the cup of his severity that he might kindly show to me what I would be when only he remains in my calamity. Unkindly he has kindly shown that he was not my hope alone."—John Piper

John Piper is correct: unkindly He kindly shows us that our hope is not in the Lord alone. God created us for this one purpose: to worship the Lord God alone and perchance we put any other gods before Him or equal to Him, He will act upon us.

Having mixed motives is not necessarily your fault. You were born that way. To worship other gods or to want different outcomes more than wanting the Lord most of all is part of human cursedness. It does not make you odd but normal.

No matter how hard we try, we cannot get out of our way, which is why we need the Lord, not just for our salvation but also for our sanctification. Mercifully, the Lord does not leave us alone after He saves us. He stays with us, always working, sometimes hurting, but relentlessly loving us. He aims to conform us to the image of His Son —an image Adam distorted, and now, because of the gospel, there is hope for a reversal of the curse.

There is a purpose in pain. There is a reason you are going through what is happening to you. The Lord is at work for your good. Though you cannot perceive all the good He plans for your life, you must know He is active, planning, and preparing future blessing. With that in mind, here are three considerations to help you as you ponder what the Author of your life is writing into your script. As you read these things, ask the Spirit of God to open your mind to receive and respond to how you need to change.

In His Kindness, He Humbles Us

Though we do not want to hear this, the truth is that we are proud. We have a high view of ourselves, and we do not want to lower it in any way. And we want others to have a similar perspective of us. We want to be liked, received, accepted, and loved. Anything that can put us in an unfavorable light or at a disadvantage will cause us to fight back in anger or to retreat in fear.

We are most loyal to ourselves, and only the Lord can impose Himself into our lives in such a way to break us from this bondage. Suffering humbles, and being humbled is what we need the most.

- Are you being humbled by your suffering or are you resisting the Lord's suffering?
- How are you responding to your suffering: anger, fear, or faith?

In His Kindness, He Vindicates Us

During our seasons of suffering, it is not possible to see the future that will come as a result of our suffering. This problem is where we are called to trust in the active goodness of the Lord on our behalf.

If you respond with humility, rather than anger or fear, to what is happening, you will have positioned yourself for an excellent and favorable outcome. Job's vindication in chapter forty-two did not turn into vindictiveness because he accepted the humbling of the Lord. If you try to manage your pain through self-reliant means, you will not only prolong it, but you will complicate all of your relationships that are part of your suffering.

Notice the Progression: you must live in authentic humility, which means you must be pliable to the Lord's work rather than resistant to it. If you do this, you will be at rest, even in the storm (Matthew 8:23–27). This response will position you to access the Lord's strength rather than relying on yourself (2 Corinthians 1:8–9).

"He restores my soul. He leads me in paths of righteousness for his name's sake" (Psalm 23:3).

164

The Lord will restore you if you walk down the paths of right living that He provides for you, even if you find those ways laced with suffering. The reason He will restore you is that it is His name on the line, not yours. You are His child, and He is responsible for you.

The Book of Job is not a book about Job but a book about God. It was the Lord who was on trial, and it was the "retribution policy" that the devil was challenging: Job does right, and he will receive good, but if he does wrong, he will receive evil. The Lord took all Job had away, and he still held to his faith, though he suffered mightily. The Lord was proven not guilty in the matter of Job, and when the suffering was over, He vindicated His servant.

- Are you patiently trusting in the Lord's future vindication of you?
- What is it you want that keeps you from resting in the Lord and, thus, hindering His victory in your life?

In His Kindness, He Blesses Us

Be careful here. You do not want to complicate the process of suffering by being stubborn, fearful, or self-reliant. You must give yourself entirely up to God's full work in your life, or you will put yourself in opposition to His inexhaustible favor (James 4:6).

Sinning in response to the sin in your life can bring more sin down on your head, which is what Job did, and the Lord thundered down hard on him. Then Job repented, and he was eventually vindicated.

The blessing of the Lord comes through a person's willingness to die. That is one of the most influential pictures of the gospel: Jesus was fearful of the suffering that was in His future (Matthew 26:39). He did not want to experience it.

165

Finally, He did relent by giving Himself entirely over to the will of His Father. From there, things only became worse for Him. After He walked out of Gethsemane, His persecutors nailed Him to a tree.

Do you want to be blessed? Of course, you do. Do not be deceived about how blessings come. It never occurred to me how the loss of everything that was dear to me in 1988 was the beginning of profound and undeserved benefits that could only come through the door of suffering.

1. How are you responding to your suffering? What does your response to your suffering reveal about how you think about the Lord?

2. Are you confident the Lord is going to bless you and out of that confidence (faith) you're experiencing soul stabilization?

3. How do you need to rethink the suffering the Lord has brought to you, and in what practical ways do you need to change?

Chapter 17

When God Does Not Act Like You

When things do not go according to your plans and the losses keep mounting, it's only a short step from walking away from God and caring friends who can persevere with you and your suffering.

Reality

Each of us will lose everyone and everything that is in our lives. Except for Christ, there is nothing we will gain that we will not lose. From a Christian worldview, this news does not have to be spiritually debilitating.

"Indeed, I count everything as loss because of the surpassing worth of knowing Christ Jesus my Lord. For his sake I have suffered the loss of all things and count them as rubbish, in order that I may gain Christ" (Philippians 3:8).

The loss of all things happens incrementally throughout our lives until the very end when we lose the last of all that we possess, which is life itself. Though this is a dark way to introduce a chapter, it may do some of us, particularly those who hold too tightly to what they cannot control, some good to reenter reality.

The central question to interact with is how you are responding to the slow and incremental death of all things. What kind of death is currently happening in your life? How are you losing your grip on the things you cherish? What losses are you accumulating?

Sin is the tsunami that eventually runs over everything. Because of the law of "cause and effect," there is no other option. Adam sinned against the Ruler of the universe and because of his offense, death entered into our experience (Romans 5:12). I am not only talking about the finality of death but the deteriorating effect of death that comes into our lives. Marriages that began well slowly die if they drift from the rejuvenating power of the gospel. Families split apart because of sin. Relationships break down because of a lack of gospel intentionality.

Death has many shades from which nobody escapes: the impact is on all of us. When that which once was is no longer yours, how do you respond? This fact is the ultimate, unavoidable, and inevitable question that forces you to look in the mirror to accurately examine the authenticity of your faith.

Reaction

Sometimes we can want something so badly that we unwittingly embark on a process of blinding ourselves to how much power that thing has over us. This "blind spot" is what was happening to Job. It is essential to interject here that Job was an extremely good man. After you juxtapose his legitimate goodness to how blind he became, you can get a sense of how the power of sin had captivated his mind.

The incredibly righteous Job was swirling down the drain of life, grabbing at the air, while his friends were giving him bad advice. After thirty-seven chapters of fruitless groping at the darkness with his friends, Job had wholly given in to the justification of his actions, even by blaming God.

There are times in our lives when we can want something so much that we turn to blaming God for not giving it to us. And like Job, our blame is not always obvious. I have done this a few times while caught in unmitigated suffering.

For the longest time with Job, it seemed more like it was just a battle between friends who disputed theological ideas. Job's friends were making some poor observations, and he became sinfully angry. Whenever we choose anger in response to those who disappoint us, there is something more profound that is going wrong in our lives. Sinful reactions are an indication that something is amiss with our experience with the Lord.

People accused Jesus of many things that were not true, but He never resorted to sinful anger to make His points. The reason Job became sinful was because there was something more meaningful to him than finding shalom from God's sovereign care. The Lord affirmed this when He asked Job, "Will you even put me in the wrong? Will you condemn me that you may be on the right?" (Job 40:8) Job's mind had become so twisted that he was willing to blame God to access what he wanted.

1. **Reality** – The reality is Job lost some things he loved.
2. **Reaction** – His reaction became sinful anger, even to the point of twisted justifications.
3. **Reason** – The reason was that Job was afraid.

Reason

When you are dealing with an angry person and you want to know what is driving the individual, open the door to his heart. There you will find your answer. The number one thing that churns sinful anger in the soul is fear, and that is what was driving Job.

He was afraid.

He was afraid of losing what meant most to him. The truth is that he had already lost most of those things he loved, e.g., family, wealth, and health. But all was not lost, and he was going to fight to the bitter end to keep from losing the final paltry remnants of his life. And the last thing left on Job's ledger was his (self) righteousness. Though he had lost everything else, he was not going to give up the rightness of his position, even if it meant a "perspective change" on how he viewed the Lord.

Suffering—which easily tempts us to fear—can cause us to change our thinking about life, God, and others. Job did this. He was losing touch with reality as evidenced by his growing inability to no longer see what he needed to see.

Fearfulness is the one motive of the heart that we do not want to openly and honestly discuss. We would instead create and perpetuate drama in our lives than deal honestly with our fears in the context of our community. An unwillingness to deal with our fearful motives that are creating a war in our hearts (James 4:1–3) will never bring you to the Lord's solution. Ongoing fear will perpetuate anger, which will alienate the sufferer from God and his community.

Dilemma

This kind of stubbornness creates a dilemma for those who desire to care for the hurting person. Once you put your finger on their fear—the fear of what they do not want to lose—they may bite your finger and sever the relationship. This tension has been my biggest dilemma when caring for others. At some point, you have to identify their fear and try to help them walk through what is controlling them. If the fear is too deep and their love for what they are losing is too captivating, they will retaliate with anger.

As a wife said, "I don't care about Christ and his suffering, I just want my husband to love me." Her fear of not being loved the way she wanted her husband to love her altered how she thought about God and me. And she did not hold back her anger as I tried to reorient her thinking to a higher plane and different kind of trust in the Lord.

Though Job's friends offered partially poor counsel—the only kind humans can give—Job became arrogant and angry, and he retaliated by spewing self-justifications for his actions. Job was not being wise but selfish. He wanted what he wanted, and he would find no consolation in anything else. And if anyone challenged his thinking, there would be retribution because Job was not a humble man. He was going to have what he wanted, and there were no other considerations.

His stubborn refusal is why the Lord stepped into the situation. Job could talk others down: he could put them in their place. His combination of theological knowledge, the gift of argumentation, and selfish motives were formidable. Job was too smart to be assailable. Then there was the Lord.

Job ran his mouth just long enough to call down the thunder of the Lord on his self-righteous and angry whining. Though he could blow others off by his pedantic verbosity, he was not going to move God. The Lord made sure of this by stacking the cards against Job. You can read His speech in Job 38–41. When we refuse to listen to the appeals of others, there is no other place for the Christian to go but to the court of the Lord.

Response

"How am I to trust God when God does not act the way I think He should?"

Job was engaging God through the lens of justice rather than the lens of wisdom. He was more concerned with fairness than sovereign wisdom. When this happens, there is a good chance a person will shipwreck his religion, life, and relationships.

Wisdom is the ability to look behind what is happening on the surface of your life and to trust that God is working out His wise and good plans for you, even if it makes no sense. Job's interest in justice hid his need for wisdom. We are like this, too. When someone hurts us or disappoints us, how quick are we to retaliate with anger because we want justice? The reasoning goes like this: sin must be punished, and if he has done wrong, I must give him a piece of my mind.

Or, she hurt my feelings. She did not give me what I hoped for, and now I am going to pout until she gives me what I need. Pouting is anger turned inward, which usually leads to manipulation, or anger turned outward.

It is so easy to play the "justice card" when things are not going our way while missing the "wisdom card" that speaks of a loving and sovereign Lord who is always working for our good (Romans 8:28). Whatever is under your suffering is under the Lord's control. He is in complete charge of your life. Though the reality of death's shadow, mentioned at the beginning of this chapter, is accurate and powerful, there is one thing that is stronger (2 Corinthians 1:8–9).

"Who has first given to me, that I should repay him? Whatever is under the whole heaven is mine" (Job 41:11).

If you have a God who is wise enough and powerful enough to be mad at because He is not stopping the suffering in your life, isn't it also true that you have a God who is wise enough and powerful enough to have reasons for allowing it, even though you cannot understand?

You do not live in a gospel-less world. One of the reasons we become so miserable and angry when suffering comes is because we assume we are supposed to understand how God should be working in our lives. The gospel is more counter-intuitive than you ever imagined.

Only the Lord can use sin sinlessly. Look at the cross to remind yourself of this truth. A real and loving God will not elevate your wishes for what you think needs to be done when suffering is the best way to accomplish what needs to be done. Similarly, a wise, courageous, and loving friend will not cave to the sufferer but will love the friend, which may mean drawing out the "disguised fears" that perpetuate the suffering the person so desperately wants to end.

Call to Action

If you believe the Lord should have kept your suffering from you, then you have a small God. If you think your friends should not press into your life to help you work through your disappointments, you have a small view of friendships.

A small God and small friendships have this one thing in common: it allows you to be in control. You can keep your fears hidden while justifying your actions with arguments if you keep your friends and your God pushed away from the actual motives of your heart. Are you self-aware enough to see how your fears are motivating you not to trust the Lord and to drift from the community?

It is rare for a person not to be self-aware of some of their fears. In most cases, they are aware enough but are unwilling to be transparent about what is going on in their lives. I am not sure how self-aware Job was about his hidden fears.

It would be an argument from silence to speculate about how dialed-in he was to his heart motives. Perhaps you are like this, in that you are not fully aware how fear has gripped your heart as you think about your suffering. One of the easiest ways to diagnose how fear has captivated your heart is how you respond to your suffering.

1. When you think about what you may be losing, how do you respond?
2. Do you become angry at God and others?
3. When someone begins to address your fears, do you sin by lying, worrying, or becoming angry?

If you will openly talk about your fears, while seeking help from your friends to trust the Lord, you are heading in the right direction. If you will not do this, blindness has already begun to dull your mind.

Chapter 18

You Know Your Faith Is Real When

Job's wild ride through the crucible of suffering was coming to an end. The devil was defeated. The Lord was glorified. And Job changed. I knew the first two things were going to happen: Satan would lose, and God would win.

What I did not expect was all the Lord wanted to do with Job. I did not even know he had a problem. He seemed to be a good man, going about doing good (Job 1:1, 5). And after Satan turned his world upside down, he refused to sin or charge the Lord with any wrong (Job 1:22).

Leave it to the Lord to go deeper. He always goes farther than anyone else and does more than what is expected (Isaiah 55:8–9; Ephesians 3:20). What we anticipate Him to do is not always what He does.

What we do not conceive as a possibility, He accomplishes. Though it was assumed He would win the bet with the devil, I did not expect a radical and more profound transformation of Job.

If the extent of the story was about a wager, there was nothing more to write after the first chapter. Job was laid low by the Lord, and he responded with humility and praise (Job 1:20–22). This reaction is what the devil said would not happen, but it is what the Lord knew would happen (Job 1:8–12).

But God knew more than the rest of us. This story was not just between the Lord and Satan. The Lord loved Job and wanted him to have a broader experience of faith. Being a good man was not enough. There was something amiss in Job's heart, and the Lord wanted to adjust it.

Just before the final curtain fell, we learned how there was one more piece of work the Lord needed to do for Job. It was a test. The time to put up or shut up had come. He testified how he was of small account (Job 40:4). Job claimed that he had changed (Job 42:5–6). But the reality of his testimony needed validating by a practical exam.

One More Thing

After four years of crawling through the dirt with Job, I felt as though I had changed, too. Before God radically and terribly imposed Himself upon me, I was living a decent life. Then, without warning, I was crushed beyond my worst fears.

I crumbled and grumbled, eventually giving up on God. Mercifully, He would not let go of me. He persevered when I would not. He loved me enough to allow the suffering to change me. He slowly and carefully whittled me down to size.

Toward the end of this horrible experience, I finally repented. I, like Job, had heard of the Lord by the hearing of the ear, but now I could perceive Him in a new and transforming way (Job 42:5–6). Still, there was one more thing to do.

Was the Lord's "internal heart-work" real, or was I trying to manipulate God and others by saying I was fine when I was not? Had I been truly and effectually changed? There was only one way to tell. I needed to "road test" my supposed transformation.

Enduring through horrible circumstances is a good thing, but the most authentic assessment of the Lord's work in your life is how you respond to life's challenges.

The test the Lord gave me was straightforward. It came in the form of a few questions He proposed to me. The query was designed to reveal my practical awareness of the gospel as well as my willingness to live it out before others.

- **Heart Question:** Was I willing to forgive those who had sinned against me (Luke 23:34)?
- **Serving Question:** Would I cooperate with the Lord by being used to help those who purposely hurt me (Mark 10:45)?

Love Your Enemies?

"And the LORD restored the fortunes of Job, when he had prayed for his friends. And the LORD gave Job twice as much as he had before" (Job 42:10).

The test for Job was also straightforward: would he pray for those who were mean to him?

The most accurate test of a person's faith is when he can demonstrate the love of God toward the person who has sinned against him (Romans 5:8). This kind of demonstration is an authentic replication of the gospel—Christ becoming a man to die for those who had sinned against Him (Luke 23:34; 2 Corinthians 5:21; Philippians 2:5–11).

"Love your enemies, do good to those who hate you, bless those who curse you, pray for those who abuse you. If you love those who love you, what benefit is that to you? For even sinners love those who love them. And if you do good to those who do good to you, what benefit is that to you? For even sinners do the same. But love your enemies, and do good. And your reward will be great, and you will be sons of the Most High, for he is kind to the ungrateful and the evil. Be merciful, even as your Father is merciful" (Luke 6:27–36).

Job passed this test, and his reward was great (Job 42:10–17). His response to his friends convicted me. I had to do what he did. The Lord blessed me with an absurd amount of personal suffering, and He called me to prove to Him if I had learned how to walk in the steps of His Son (1 Peter 2:21).

Like an unending game of Monopoly, I knew if I would not humble myself and forgive those who hurt me—at least in my heart—and attempt to serve them, my captivity would continue.

Who Do You Love?

* Have you learned the lesson of Job?
* Can you love the person who annoys you?

These are self-assessment questions. Your answers will reveal to what degree you have been affected and changed by the gospel. The call to love the unlovable is more than a nice biblical truth you should affirm. It is the gospel.

The King James Bible says the Lord turned the "captivity of Job" when he prayed for his friends. Job was in captivity. His world had fallen apart, and his soul was torn asunder. The purpose of this divine-inspired, human rigmarole was to change Job. To not change is to choose unending captivity.

- Are you aware how ongoing bitterness, anger, and unforgiveness toward someone will prolong your captivity?
- Do you know how a bad attitude toward any person who has hurt you, no matter how legit the hurt was, will push you deeper into your captivity?

The Lord wanted to release Job from his captivity, but it was up to Job if he wanted to experience release. This possibility is fantastic news in that Job held the key to his captivity, which was in his heart.

In time, I learned the lesson of Job. My incarceration ended after I repented of my self-righteous anger toward those who hurt me while seeking their forgiveness. My freedom was not in their hands. I was not a victim of my circumstances. I was a victim of the anger and self-righteousness that I carried in my heart. I was a victim of me.

"When" Will This Happen?

The authentication of your Christian maturity is not how you are coping with your problems, but it is how you are loving and serving others—particularly those who have hurt you. Some could wrongly surmise that Job was transformed from a counseling perspective because he had been through the grist mill with God and had come out on the other end loving God.

Enduring suffering and loving God is not the best assessment of a Christian's maturity. The comprehensiveness of Job's total makeover would be determined by how he responded to the Lord's request to love others more than himself (Matthew 22:37–39). The power of the gospel is useless if we don't effectually apply it to those who need it, especially those who hurt us.

"Do nothing from rivalry or conceit but in humility count others more significant than yourselves" (Philippians 2:3).

Job's friends hurt him. As you read their dialogue, your heart aches for him. Much of what they said made them careless and unkind counselors. This relational problem is what makes the Lord's request for Job to pray for them all the more powerful, purposeful, and practical.

It was showtime, and Job had an immediate opportunity to put his newly reframed theology to practice. And he did not disappoint: he prayed for his friends. Job humbly and obediently went from being a disputing Christian to an interceding Christian. This transition from being incarcerated by self-righteousness to being freed through genuine humility happened when Job prayed for his friends. The word "when" is an element of time.

- Your captivity will end when . . .
- He changed when . . .

You can pray for change until you are blue in the face. You can talk about all the Lord has done for you until the cows come home. You can affirm the many principles of the Bible, but the proof is in the pudding. It is "when" you act upon what you know that you will experience the liberating power of the gospel.

Words! Words! Words!

In the Broadway musical *My Fair Lady* the character Eliza Doolittle became more than a little agitated when her beau was slow about showing his affections for her. He was doing more talking than doing. She rebuked him this way:

> *Words! Words! Words! I'm so sick of words!*
> *I get words all day through;*
> *First from him, now from you!*
> *Is that all you blighters can do?*
> *Don't talk of stars burning above;*
> *If you're in love, Show me!*

James, the half-brother of Jesus, was a little more direct than even the sharped-tongues Eliza Doolittle. He said it this way:

"So whoever knows the right thing to do and fails to do it, for him it is sin" (James 4:17).

It will not do to give intellectual affirmation to what you need to do. As Eliza said, "Show me!" As James said, "Faith without works is dead." (James 2:17)

You will not benefit from the blessings of the Lord if you are holding unresolved conflict in your relationships. This hard truth makes "when" a big word. It cannot be faked, manipulated, or contrived. God knows every thought and intention of your heart (Hebrews 4:12–13). Can you freely pray for and actively serve those who have hurt you?

My question is not theoretical. It is a practical question that strikes at the heart of your understanding and application of the gospel in your life. If you cannot forgive or if you persist in holding resentment, anger, and hostility toward others, your religion is marginalized, if it is real at all. The point of Job's journey and the accusation of the devil was whether or not he would prove his faith—would he love God regardless of his circumstances?

The Questioner Turns to You

To what degree is your faith governed by what you get from the Lord? And, are you able to bless the Lord when you don't receive what you want? (See Job 1:20–23.) Take a moment to think about your friends. Maybe it is a spouse, parent, child, relative, co-worker, church friend, or former friend.

- Have any of them hurt you?
- If so, are you free from what they did to you, to where you can be practically and measurably redemptive toward them?

Truest Test of Christianity

Christ, the offended, engaged the offenders so that He could transform them. He did this for you and me, which is your calling. Modeling the gospel is Christian maturity. God will release you from your captivity when you can actively love those who have hurt you.

"Then Satan answered the LORD and said, 'Does (put your name here) fear God for no reason? Have you not put a hedge around him and his house and all that he has, on every side? You have blessed the work of his hands, and his possessions have increased in the land. But stretch out your hand and touch all that he has, and he will curse you to your face'" (Job 1:9–11).

Call to Action

1. What was the main thing the Lord pinpointed in your life from reading this chapter?
2. Will you write out your specific plan for change? Be brief but detailed.
3. Will you share with a friend what the Lord taught you, asking your friend to help you change?

If you are still captivated by unresolved bitterness, anger, cynicism, or unforgiveness, I appeal to you to go back to the beginning of this chapter and reread it, asking the Lord to release you from the captivation of your heart.

Chapter 19

A Note to Job's Friends

Dear Rick,

How do you encourage someone toward the Lord when they are angry at God for past difficulties? They are mad because God did not protect them or deliver them from their problems.

When Job questioned God, the Lord responded with answers like, "Where were you when I laid the foundation of the earth? Tell me, if you have understanding. Shall a faultfinder contend with the Almighty? He who argues with God, let him answer it."

This kind of response allowed Job to see because he was not able to make a proper judgment of what had happened to him. Then Job put his hand over his mouth and said,

"Behold, I am of small account; what shall I answer you? I have spoken once, and I will not answer; twice, but I will proceed no further" (Job 40:4).

I believe Scripture teaches that God owes us nothing. He has given us everything in Christ, and if we start with that premise, our hearts are humbled. Is this the wrong direction to take with someone who has suffered repeated hurtful things at the hands of others?

We have spent weeks on God's love towards her that is in Christ, yet she still holds such anger against God. I know you said it takes a long time for hurting individuals to work through their issues. I so long to see my friend set free from the torment.

When Friends Suffer

You are on the right track with her, so don't deviate from where you want to go. She needs to know about the love of God, and she needs to move forward in her thinking and living. Eventually. And, as you have surmised, it will be a long time before you can get her to that place in her experience.

Of course, you cannot predict when she will arrive. To be honest with you, she may never come to that better place. It's not your call. Only the Lord holds this kind of information (Deuteronomy 29:29). Her future life is in His mind, and He will not share those intentions with you (Hebrews 4:12-13). His desire for you is to faithfully serve her as she wrestles through the torturous torment of what has happened to her.

Be sure that you don't put time limits on her. Counseling can have limitations, especially if there is a prescribed number of sessions in view. You cannot mandate change or write out a timeline for specific expectations that she must meet.

When the Storm Comes

You may be surprised to know that many Christians are angry at God, though I suspect most of them would never admit it. I would not recommend for anyone to openly talk about their anger at God, just as they should not talk about their anger with anyone–if talking about their anger is all they are going to do.

In your situation with your friend, admitting her struggle with the Sovereign Lord is a positive. The fact she will go there with you is what any angry person should do. It is helpful for compassionate and competent friends to know the internal turmoil of others. For this, I am grateful you have this opportunity with her.

I'm sure she is aware of the sovereignty of God, to some degree. She is probably aware of His omnipotent ability and His presence everywhere. When she factors these things into her thinking, it is reasonable for her to ponder, "Where was God when all this crazy stuff went down in my life?" I've thought similarly.

April 08, 1988 was the day my wife of nine years decided to leave me with our two young children. They never returned. More than three decades later I'm still affected by what began on that day. A dark cloud rolled over my life and never left. During the early years, I spent a considerable amount of time reading the Book of Job. He became my constant companion.

"Why is light given to a man whose way is hidden, whom God has hedged in? For my sighing comes instead of my bread, and my groanings are poured out like water. For the thing that I fear comes upon me, and what I dread befalls me. I am not at ease, nor am I quiet; I have no rest, but trouble comes" (Job 3:23-26).

Job said the thing he had feared had come upon him (Job 3:25). I'm not sure if that has ever happened to you. It did for me. What she is going through cannot be thoroughly explained or understood unless you have been in her place and experienced a comparable pain. This perspective does not disqualify you from helping her, but I do want to call attention to the complicatedness of her situation.

Similarly, she does not fully understand the complexity of what has happened to her. How could she? Who can know the mind of the Lord? This reality is part of her problem. She does not fully understand her trouble or her God. Nobody can, not entirely.

There is an element of faith we are called to walk, and when things like what happened to her come, it can disrupt our faith in proportion to the size of the trouble. Her problems are mountainous, which means her ability to trust God will be proportionally challenging.

Ideal, but Not a Template

God's counsel to Job was perfect because God is perfect. He knew what Job needed during that "counseling season," which lasted for forty-two chapters. Please remember that we are not aware of the actual counseling time from the beginning of Job's ordeal to the end.

The part of the Lord's counsel that you have pinpointed is appropriate for your friend at some juncture in the process. I do not know when that time will be. Yes, it is a goal to aim for, but it may not be the right thing to say now. I remember a couple of times when someone gave me Romans 8:28 as part of their counsel.

That passage presents beautiful counsel to the afflicted, but my heart was not in the place to receive it. In fact, my response to "and you know how all things work together for good" was along these lines:

"Has it ever occurred to you that I might not want all things to work together for good? What I want is my family back. I'm not interested in what the Lord is trying to do in my life."

My friend gave good counsel to me, but it was the wrong time. I was talking with a sick friend who was telling me how some people are so "blessed" by her suffering. She understands what they are trying to say and she also understands how difficult it is to speak into an unchangeable situation like hers. She added, somewhat humorously, but truthfully,

"I don't want to be the poster girl for sickness so others can be grateful for their health or be encouraged by my illness. I'd rather they find another way to be grateful and encouraged."

She realizes her attitude is wrong, but she is also trying to be honest about what is going on in her thought life. I'm not trying to change my friend. I'm trying to be a friend to my friend. I want to walk with her and her husband through her unchangeable situation.

We are at the place where I can call attention to her attitude when it needs adjusting, and she receives my corrections with grace, but I can't change her or her situation, and I don't try to. Your friend is being honest with what she is thinking, and she is sharing those things with you. In that, you can find encouragement.

Counseling Is Conditional

The Book of Job is not a one-size-fits-all template for how you do things or how things will always conclude for troubled souls. The book was a unique historical moment between a man and his Creator. Not all counseling situations play out that way, though it would be nice if they did. You said,

"I believe Scripture teaches that God owes us nothing. He has given us everything in Christ, and if we start with that premise, our hearts are humbled."

This worldview is correct, but the big operative word here is "if." "If our hearts are humble" is the key. Job eventually had a humble heart, and his humility set the stage for how he responded to the strong and hard counsel given to him, which began like this:

"Then the LORD answered Job out of the whirlwind and said: "Who is this that darkens counsel by words without knowledge?" (Job 38:1-2).

I do not know your friend or where she is as far as being humble (or proud). That is not a judgment I can make. However, you must try to discern where she is at this point in her journey with the Lord. If there is resistance to God, for whatever reason, tread carefully. Let me put it this way: if she is not in chapter 38, where the Lord began to counsel Job, it's not the time for you to advise her the way He counseled Job.

Counseling is conditional on the heart of the person you're counseling. The Lord knew Job was ready to gird up his loins and receive some stern and direct counsel. It worked, and Job experienced transformation.

As you know, the Lord grants repentance (2 Timothy 2:25). We do not. We see this gift given to Job as we read his book. People are different, and each person needs counseling according to who they are and where they are, not who we think they should be or according to other people we know or even historical figures we find in the Bible.

I know you know this and I'm preaching to the choir, but a good reminder does not hurt. Your friend needs your love through care and discernment. Sometimes she needs your admonition. Most of all she needs your friendship.

I do not know how the "42 chapters" of trouble will play out for her. She may never come to the place of seeing what Job saw or responding the way Job did (Job 42:5-6, 10).

She may always be angry with the Lord. Maybe in fifteen years or so she will make some significant changes. These possibilities are in the Lord's mind. They are His secrets (Deuteronomy 29:29). You will need to become comfortable with this mystery while guarding your heart against thinking how you believe things should be is how things will be (James 4:13-17; Matthew 6:34).

Be Patient Above All Things

Patience will be your primary need as you serve her (1 Thessalonians 5:14). Soul care is some of the most laborious work there is, especially when the individuals we love don't seem to want to change—or when they are stuck, and though they would like to change, they just can't.

One thing that makes our work difficult is not being the ones who control the change process. We are the Lord's water boys and girls, faithfully watering and sowing while asking the Father to provide the growth (1 Corinthians 3:5-7). In this way, it is similar to parenting or any other relationship.

For now, you keep on plowing. Keep sowing. Be patient. Be encouraged. Live with the future expectation of the Lord restoring your friend (Psalm 23:3; Philippians 1:6). It may come while you are working with her. It may not.

"And the LORD restored the fortunes of Job, when he had prayed for his friends. And the LORD gave Job twice as much as he had before" (Job 42:10).

If she has any theological moorings at all, she probably knows the Lord is good, and He was there in her suffering, and He is working a good plan for her life now. I had limited awareness of this truth when my pain was most acute.

But there was nothing I could do to change my thinking or my hurt. It was something I had to experience through painful perseverance. No matter how many times I cried, my pain and my circumstance never changed. Finally, out of sheer desperate torment, I blurted out my anger to the Lord. I don't recommend this, but it does happen.

If you or any other person had shown up during that time, there would have been nothing you could do for me, other than be my praying, caring, persevering friend. I could not change. I was stuck.

That was a long time ago. The residual effect of that suffering lingers today but in a different way. The good Lord turned my captivity from bitter hopelessness to a ministry that helps people like your friend. I'm glad you are there for her, and in some small way, I can serve her through you. That, my friend, is what makes all my suffering worth it.

About the Author

Rick Thomas has been training in the Upstate of South Carolina since 1997. After several years as a counselor and pastor, he founded and launched his training organization to encourage and equip people for effective living.

In the early '90s, he earned a BA in Theology. Later he received a BS in Education. Rick became ordained into Christian ministry in 1993, and in 2000, he graduated with an MA in Counseling. The Association of Certified Biblical Counselors recognized him as a Fellow in 2006.

Today his organization reaches people in every country through training, blogging, podcasting, counseling, and coaching. His cyber home is RickThomas.Net.

Join Our Team

Our community is a gathering of individuals from all over the world who are seeking to live more productive and inspiring lives. We all have situational and relational challenges that could benefit from having other people bringing insight and care. Caring for others is what our community does best.

Community Resources

- Access to a stocked library of content written from a God-centered, others-centered perspective
- Live and archived webinars
- Training presentations, videos, infographics, mind maps, best practices, and more
- Private membership-only forum for questions and answers about life and relationships
- Opportunities to ask Rick and his team key questions that are important to you
- A 24/7 all-access "life coach" for personal development and training of others
- A self-paced Mastermind Training Program: Distance Education

Partner with Us

We are a membership-supported community. You can also partner with us by making a one-time or recurring donation. We are a 501(c) 3 NPO. Go to our ministry website, RickThomas.Net, to learn more.